JEWISH LONDON
AN ILLUSTRATED HISTORY

JEWISH HISTORY in London properly begins with the arrival of a small group of Jews with William the Conqueror. Despite their expulsion in 1290, the influence of Jews on the life of the capital has grown, especially after the large-scale immigrations of the 19th and 20th century. The Jews have had an extraordinary impact on the life of the city, and this book shows how it happened.

Gerry Black recalls the origins and motives of the generations of Jews who came to make their home in London. The development of the famously close-knit societies they formed in the East End, in north London and elsewhere in the capital is recorded, and illustrated, in graphic detail. He also gives a fascinating account of their struggle to establish themselves in the city – their housing, their work and trades, schools, hospitals and synagogues.

His narrative gives a vivid portrait of outstanding individuals who made notable contributions to the Jewish community and to the wider history of the capital – businessmen, artists, lawyers, artisans. At the same time he records momentous events that marked the course of Jewish history in the city, from the expulsion of 1290 to the Jack the Ripper case and the Sydney Street siege.

The story comes right up to the present day. Gerry Black looks back at the further immigration that took place from Germany and Austria before World War Two and from Egypt, Hungary, Iraq, Iran and India after the war. His lively account offers a sharp insight into the contribution made by modern Jews to the culture and economy of London. His book will be essential reading for everyone who is interested in the Jewish community and in the cultural diversity of the capital.

DR GERRY BLACK has made a special study of London's history and the history of the Jews in London in particular. His previous publications include *Lord Rothschild and the Barber: The Struggle to Establish the London Jewish Hospital* (2000), *J.F.S: The History of the Jews' Free School, London Since 1732* (1998), *Living Up West: Jewish Life in London's West End* (1994), and *Lender to the Lords, Giver to the Poor* (1992) a biography of the Victorian philanthropist, Samuel Lewis.

JEWISH LONDON
AN ILLUSTRATED HISTORY

Dr Gerry Black

Tymsder Publishing

Tymsder Publishing
PO Box 16039
London NW3 6WL
Tel/Fax 0207 372 9015
www.tymsder.co.uk

First published by Breedon Books Publishing Company Limited in 2003
Paperback edition 2007
This edition by Tymsder Publishing 2009

For my grandchildren

ISBN 978-0-953110-49-0

Produced by The Studio Publishing Services Ltd
www.publishingservicesuk.co.uk
e-mail: studio@publishingservicesuk.co.uk

Printed in Great Britain

Contents

Preface

EVER since the first Jewish community settled in England during the reign of William the Conqueror, approximately two-thirds of British Jews have lived in London. The history of Anglo-Jewry is therefore largely reflected in the history of the Jews of London.

There are excellent books available on the history of British Jewry dealing with Britain as a whole, with particular periods or events, with individuals, institutions, and some with provincial towns. There is, however, no book devoted to Jewish London continuously from 1070 to the present day, and that, in a modest way, is the gap that this book aims to fill.

Jews today account for between two and three percent of the population of Greater London (less than one percent in Britain as a whole), but London and its Jewish residents have each influenced the other to an extent greater than mere numbers suggest. With the exception of the mediaeval period, during which the Jews suffered greatly, both parties have benefited from the association.

To cover more than 900 years in a short book obviously involves selection, and no two authors would make exactly the same choice. I have attempted to give an overall picture that accurately gives the flavour of the passing times, and ask forbearance from those whose favourite characters, institutions or events have not been included.

I should like to thank most sincerely my friends Barbara and Malcolm Brown, John Cooper, and Dr Michael Jolles for kindly reading the manuscript, and David Jacobs for his assistance with the photographs. Above all, my thanks to my wife Anita who has assisted at every stage of the work. It goes without saying that all errors are my responsibility alone.

Map of the East End of London in 1900 showing Jewish residents in proportion to the total population; in some streets 100 percent.

JEWISH EAST LONDON

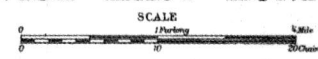

SCALE

This Map shows by Colour the proportion of the Jewish population to other residents of East London, street by street, in 1899.

EXPLANATION OF COLOURING.

Proportion of Jews indicated.

- 95% to 100%.
- 75% and less than 95%.
- 50% and less than 75%.
- 25% and less than 50%.
- 5% and less than 25%.
- Less than 5% of Jews.

NOTE.—In all streets coloured blue the Jews form a majority of the inhabitants; in those coloured red, the Gentiles predominate.

(From Russell & Lewis The Jew in London)

Chapter 1

1070–1290: The first Jewish Londoners

THE Jews have never accounted for more than one per cent of the population of Britain. There were individuals or small groups of Jews living in England in Roman and Saxon times, but it was only after William the Conqueror arrived that the first Jewish community settled there.

Normandy, William's home country, was prosperous, partly thanks to a body of Jews who contributed greatly to its wealth. They were able to do so because under the laws of the mediaeval Catholic church Christians were banned from lending at interest, it being declared a sin. This, coupled with the virtual exclusion of the Jews in northern Europe from all other trades and handicrafts, apart from the practice of medicine, compelled them to devote themselves more and more to moneylending and commerce. William believed they could be a key to making his newly-acquired land equally prosperous. In around 1070 he invited a group of Jews to London from Rouen. They brought with them some capital and their commercial experience.

During the following 220 years the Jews of England endured a roller-coaster existence. Periods of relative success, wealth and tranquillity were followed by years during which they suffered cruelty to an extent notorious even by the standards of mediaeval Europe.

The hub of the walled City of London was Cheapside, a market street with stalls and shops on either side. For London it was, and indeed still is, a very wide thoroughfare. The Jews settled in a street running off Cheapside which adopted and still bears the name Old Jewry. The area they occupied was not large, extending perhaps just a little further to the north than where Gresham Street is now, and a little to the west and east of Old Jewry itself.

The Jews' position within English society was unique. They were not serfs bound in allegiance to their lords, nor lords bound in allegiance to the king. Instead, William took them under his direct protection, bypassing the lords, a situation that had both advantages and disadvantages. They existed entirely at the royal pleasure under charters that could be revoked at any moment. Vast sums could be extorted by any king who wished to do so, merely by declaring a 'special levy' upon the whole community. Further, and unfortunately, the promised protection was not always immediately available when needed, and not all succeeding monarchs were as favourably disposed towards Jews.

Unlike the majority of the population the Jews were allowed to travel freely throughout the country but, as in continental Europe, most trades were barred to them. They were ineligible to join the guilds that controlled the crafts since these were organised on a religious basis. They could not farm, as they were forbidden from owning land or hiring Christian labour. However, Canon Law did not apply to them and they could loan out their capital at interest. It was an occupation that could be profitable, but carried considerable risks.

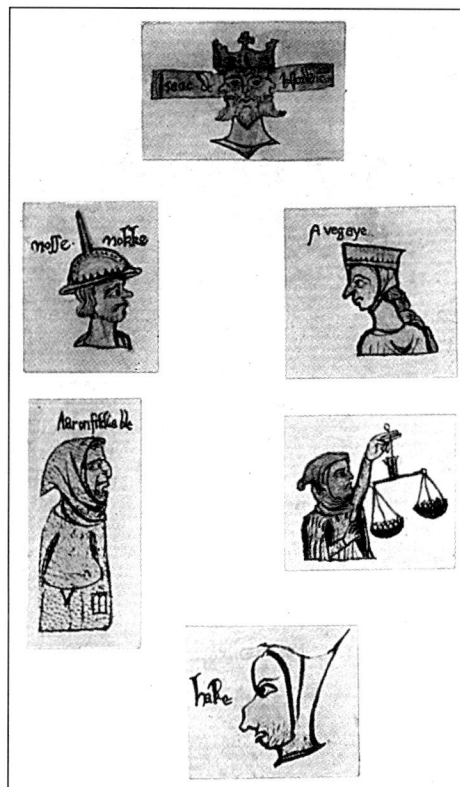

Contemporary caricatures of six mediaeval Jews.

Throughout the 12th and 13th century English monarchs were plagued by a persistent shortage of funds and borrowed from the Jews to pay for their wars, their ever more magnificent courts and buildings, and their elaborate administrations, staffed by salaried officials. The great lords loved luxury and were also big spenders. They shared with royalty the problems of a perennial shortage of cash, and they too became heavy borrowers.

As for the Church, the arrival of the Jews in England occurred just when a need arose for the erection of many important buildings devoted to religious as well as secular purposes. Without capital no large building schemes could be undertaken. Notwithstanding its attacks on usury, the church willingly and openly borrowed at interest from Jewish financiers who advanced money to abbeys and minsters, including Lincoln Cathedral, Peterborough Cathedral and Westminster Abbey, on the security of their plate.

The early years were marked by generally good relations between Christians and Jews. Though Jews often chose to live close together, there were no enforced ghettos, that is areas in which the Jews were *compelled* to live. Jews and Christians visited each other's homes, drank together, and the Jews were welcomed for their medical skills. William II (1087–1100) encouraged friendly religious debates between Jews and churchmen present at his court, jokingly promising 'by the face of Luke' to embrace Judaism should the bishops lose the argument. Perhaps fortunately for the Jews, it was adjudged that it was they who lost. Nonetheless, the insistence of the Jews on eating kosher food, worshipping separately and having their own burial places made some of the local populace generally suspicious and hostile.

Group of Christians and Jews in a public disputation of a type encouraged by William II. Note the characteristic hats worn by Jews in the Middle Ages.

By the time Henry I ascended the throne in 1100 there were up to 1,000 Jews in London. The community had been augmented a few years earlier by new arrivals who had escaped from Rouen, where crusading knights had set about butchering all Jews who refused to accept baptism. A few English Jews were by now extremely rich and able to afford stone houses. The remainder largely depended on them for their livelihood, acting as their servants or agents, and their income was modest.

The peaceful quality of the lives of Jews in England was broken in 1130 when the Jews of London were accused of killing a sick man, who perhaps had gone to one of them for medical treatment. For this, the community was fined the then enormous sum of £2,000. Worse was to follow. In 1144, the dead body of a young apprentice named William was found in a wood near Norwich. The preposterous rumour was spread that the Jews had abducted him from his family and crucified him, using his blood in their Passover ceremony. He was buried with great solemnity in Norwich Cathedral, and miracles, visions and wonderful occurrences were said to have followed. The story spread to London where angry mobs threatened the Jews, but on this occasion no serious harm befell them. It was, however, a harbinger of things to come, and similar reports surfaced in Gloucester, Bury St Edmunds and Bristol.

The most prosperous period for London's Jews was during the long reign of Henry II (1154–1189) when they and the country enjoyed peace. Unusually for the time, the Jews were almost all literate, men, women and children alike. What was particularly remarkable was the economic role played by Jewish women. There are many examples of Jewesses taking part in business on their own account and on equal terms with men, paying their taxes to the king and jealously claiming their rights – feminists centuries ahead of their time.

At the rear of St Giles and Cripplegate the community leased a plot of land called Jews' Garden for use as a cemetery. Until 1177 it was the only Jewish cemetery in England. When a death occurred, the body was transported by wagon, even from places as far away as Exeter or York. The area and the street called Jewin Street that marked the site were destroyed by bombing in World War Two and no longer exist.

On Sunday 3 September 1189, the day of Richard I's coronation, events took place that soon got seriously out of hand. Although they had been ordered to stay away, many Jews flocked to Westminster Abbey to present costly gifts to the king to display their loyalty. Some managed to slip inside but were driven away by a doorkeeper. The crowd outside became agitated, and the cry went up that the Jews had intended to harm the king. Several were beaten or trampled to death before they could escape. Exaggerated rumours spread from Westminster to the City, where it was reported that the king had given orders for the Jews to be exterminated. In their well-built stone houses they were able to resist the growing mob for some hours until, towards night-fall, a fire was deliberately started, took hold and rapidly spread. Though some managed to find refuge in the Tower of London or under the protection of friendly neighbours, several perished in their houses and others were killed when they ventured into the street. Their houses were plundered, and by the following day at least 30 Jewish men, women and children had been killed.

After Richard left for the Crusades (the Jews having been disproportionately taxed to meet the costs), a terrible tragedy occurred at York in March 1190. A body of Crusaders who were due to follow Richard, together with barons indebted to Jews, some clergymen and others envious of the Jews' wealth, conspired to kill the Jews of York. Several Jewish houses were burned to the ground and 150 fled for protection to the royal castle, where they were besieged. They were offered a means of escape – accepting baptism – but, led by their rabbi, they committed suicide rather than submit to conversion.

The mob then stole the records of debts due to Jews and destroyed them. The incident sent shockwaves through every Jewish community in the country, including, of course, London. 'No longer', wrote the chronicler William of Newburgh in his *History of English Affairs,* 'were the Jews living in that England in which their fathers had been happy and respected'.

On the death of a Jew his estate passed to the Crown, including the debts due to him. The king usually kept one third, and allowed the heirs to keep the balance so that they could continue in business and thus raise more revenue for the king. Because of the lost records at York the king had been deprived

*The earliest picture of
a Jewess in England,
1233.*

of some of his revenue. Thereafter all Jewish possessions and debts due to
them were registered and carefully safeguarded in London and other major
centres of Jewish settlement, in an institution which came to be known as the
Exchequer of the Jews. Its main purpose was to protect the king's interests,
not those of the Jews.

The barons later required King John to include a clause in the Magna Carta
to the effect that in the case of debts due from a baron to a Jew the king was
entitled to repayment of the capital debt only, not the accumulated interest.
This relief from interest payments meant that for the barons a dead Jewish
moneylender was preferable to a living one, a factor that constantly preyed on
the minds of the Jewish moneylenders and their families.

When the barons occupied London in 1215, Old Jewry was the first area
plundered and the stones of destroyed Jewish houses were used to strengthen
the City Walls. When Ludgate was replaced in 1586 a stone was uncovered
which was the tombstone of 'Rabbi Moses, the son of the Learned and Wise
Rabbi Isaac', suggesting that the Jewish cemetery had also been attacked.

Under further restrictions, Jews were not allowed to enter a church or
chapel, nor do anything to prevent other Jews from converting to Christianity.
No Christian nurse could suckle a male Jewish child, nor could Christians act
as servants to the Jews or eat in their houses. Jews were ordered not to buy
meat during Lent.

Sexual intercourse between Jews and Gentiles was forbidden. In order to avoid this happening in ignorance of the identity of the parties, the Lateran Council of 1215 pronounced that all non-Christians had to wear a distinguishing mark on their clothing. It was only after 1253 that the requirement was strictly enforced in England. Jews had to wear a piece of white cloth or parchment in the form of the legendary shape of the Two Tablets of stone containing the ten commandments. It was more strictly enforced in 1275 by Edward I, who stipulated that a piece of yellow taffeta had to be worn over his heart by every Jew over seven years of age. At the same Lateran Council it was ordered that Jews were not to be given public office. As will be seen, it was to be more than 600 years before this restriction was removed.

In around 1230, the Jews, who had until then worshipped in their homes or temporary accommodation, built themselves a synagogue, the first in London, on the north-west corner of Old Jewry and Gresham Street. (It was later seized by Henry III and donated to the monks of the order of St Anthony for use as a church). Four others followed in Threadneedle Street, Gresham Street, Coleman Street and Ironmonger Lane. Jews were required to subdue their voices during their services so that Christians might not hear them. The Wren church of St Laurence Jewry, which today stands in front of the Guildhall and is the Lord Mayor's official church, derives its name simply from being near Old Jewry.

The Domus Conversorum

To avoid the growing pressures upon them, some Jews succumbed to the temptation of conversion. In 1232, Henry II issued an order for the founding of a home for destitute Jews converted to Christianity, although it was said of him that he was really more keen to convert them into cash than into Christians. The house of a wealthy Jew living in Chancery Lane was seized for the purpose and called the 'Domus Conversorum'. There, the converts were given new non-Jewish names, taught the Christian doctrine, fed, modestly paid and protected. They were allowed to engage in the trades that had previously been closed to them and there were usually between 80 and 100 residents at any one time.

The Domus Conversorum remained open to receive baptised Jews almost without a break until the beginning of the 17th century. In 1837, the Public Record Office (now at Kew) was erected on the site. Interestingly, its first Deputy Keeper of the Records was Sir Francis Palgrave, né Cohen, and the next Master of the Rolls, who exercised judicial authority over its contents, was Sir George Jessel, the first Jewish judge.

Distribution of
THE JEWS OF ENGLAND
before the Expulsion

On 18 July 1290 Edward I decreed that all the Jews in England must leave by 1 November of that year. During their stay there had been 120 small settlements throughout the country.

The situation for Jews in England continued to deteriorate. They were taxed ever more heavily, tortured to reveal where they kept their money and imprisoned until they paid. When one 'Jew of Bristol' refused to pay his ransom King John ordered his torturers to pull out one of his molar teeth every day until he complied. He held out for seven days, but paid on the eighth. Many fled to the Continent and many, reduced to poverty and unable to escape, had to beg from door to door and according to one writer 'prowled the city like dogs'.

In 1275, three years after Edward I came to the throne, having inherited an impoverished Jewry of little further financial benefit to him, he issued a statute under the terms of which even moneylending and the practice of medicine were forbidden to Jews. In return, they were to be allowed to become farmers and artisans, the latter concession being rendered largely meaningless because of the guild system.

Both Jews and Christians were prosecuted for engaging in 'coin clipping', filing down the edges of coins, putting them back into circulation, then melting down the clippings into bullion. A drive specifically aimed at Jewish offenders was launched throughout the country in 1278 and many were imprisoned in the Tower of London. It was reported that up to 300 were hanged for the offence in London alone.

Expulsion

The situation simply could not continue and finally the axe fell. Parliament requested the expulsion of the Jews and on 18 July 1290 – which coincided with the Fast of *Tisha B'Av*, the day Jews commemorate the anniversary of the destruction of the First and Second Temples – Edward I signed a decree of expulsion. All Jews were ordered to leave the country by 1 November of that year; the penalty for not doing so was death.

Estimates of the number that left vary widely, but it now seems generally accepted that there were between 5,000 and 6,000. Although Edward instructed the sheriffs to ensure they suffered no harm on the journey they were not allowed to leave in peace, a story that was to be repeated many times over the centuries. Some were robbed of their goods. One ship's captain deliberately ran into a sandbank near Queensborough in the Thames estuary and invited the Jews to stretch their legs. They were then left to drown with the rising tide. He was later prosecuted and hanged for the offence. Even into the 20th century groups of orthodox Jews would go to the spot in boats on *Tisha B'av* and say memorial prayers for them.

The departed Jews settled mainly in France and Spain. So England, the last major European country to admit Jews, was the first to expel them. According to John Stowe, the chronicler of London, the King made 'a mighty mass of money' from the sale of their houses.

Chapter 2

1290–1656: The interregnum and the Marranos

WERE there Jews in London between 1290, the year in which they were expelled, and 1656, the year in which they returned? Exclusion was not absolute, and there was never a time when England had no Jews at all. Despite the decree of expulsion, they continued to trickle into the country.

Jews were pre-eminent in medicine in Europe and frequently served as court physicians. Magister Elias was given safe conduct to England to attend upon Edward II, and Elias Sabot from Bologna was summoned to treat Henry IV. Sabot brought with him a group of nine male Jews sufficient to enable him to form a *minyan,* the quorum required for communal worship. Richard Whittington, Lord Mayor of London, obtained permission for Samson de Mirabeau to attend upon his wife.

Many Spanish and Portuguese Jews, known as Marranos, feigned acceptance of Christianity in order to avoid the horrors of the Inquisition, but they secretly continued to practise Judaism. Some escaped overseas, mainly to Italy and North America, but a small number found their way to England. The gap left in England's finance and banking when the Jews departed in 1290 was filled by the Lombards from northern Italy (hence Lombard Street), and it is believed that some of them were Marranos.

There was a colony of secret Jews in London during the reign of Henry VIII (1485–1509) that was broken up during the reign of Mary (1553–58). When Elizabeth came to the throne in 1558, several returned to England, and there were then possibly 40 or so families living in London. Synagogue services were held privately in a house owned by one Alvaro Mendes, to whom newly arrived fugitives would come for assistance and advice.

It is likely that William Shakespeare was acquainted with members of the group, and it has been suggested that Shylock in *The Merchant of Venice* was inspired by one of them, Dr Roderigo Lopez. He qualified in Portugal and fled from the Inquisition with his wife Sarah, arriving in England in 1560. He became a member of the College of Physicians and was the first house physician at St Bartholomew's Hospital. He treated Sir Francis Walsingham, the Earl of Leicester and, in 1586, the queen herself. He took part in political affairs, perhaps too much so, for there was a dreadful ending to his life. His previous patron, the Earl of Essex, the queen's favourite, turned against him and Lopez found himself charged with treason, allegedly having plotted to poison the queen. He confessed when shown the instruments of torture, but retracted the confession at his trial. As that was presided over by Essex, he was inevitably found guilty and sentenced to be hung, drawn and quartered, a penalty carried out at Tyburn on 7 June 1594.

Elizabeth had refrained from signing the death warrant for some time, and must have entertained doubts about his conviction, or at least retained some feelings of affection for him, for she did not claim her right to the condemned man's property. With the exception of a ring, said to have been given to him by the King of Spain, which Elizabeth wore to her death, she allowed his widow to retain the remainder of his estate.

Two further leading Marranos were Hector Nunez (1521–91), a distinguished doctor, who came to London in 1550 and was admitted a Fellow of the Royal College of Physicians and the College of Surgeons, and Fernandez Carvajal. Nunez lived and practised in Mark Lane and later engaged in commerce on a large scale. He had correspondents throughout Europe, and gave the English Government valuable information during the critical years of its great struggle with Spain. It was he who gave the first intelligence that the Spanish Armada had set off from Lisbon bound for England.

Carvajal (1590–1659) escaped from the Portuguese Inquisition, prospered in the Canary Islands, then settled in Leadenhall Street in London in about 1635. He owned several merchant vessels and was appointed one of the five contractors who supplied corn to the Army. In 1645 he was informed against for not attending church, but the House of Lords, on the petition of several leading London merchants, quashed the proceedings. In 1650, when war broke out with Portugal, his ships were exempted from seizure even though he was nominally a Portuguese subject. He and his sons were granted denizenship as English subjects.

Oliver Cromwell (1599–1658)

Cromwell was extremely liberal for the age in which he lived. In 1654 he wrote to Cardinal Mazarin:

I desire from my heart, I have prayed for it, I have waited for the day to see union and right understanding between Godly people – Scots, English, Jews, Gentiles, Presbyterians, Independents, Anabaptists and all.

Cromwell aimed to make England a great nation, prosperous and free. He knew that commercial expansion was essential, and believed England would benefit from having Jewish merchants on her soil. By the time of his protectorate there was a small colony of about 200 Marranos in London, all prosperous merchants, living in the eastern part of the City: in Leadenhall Street, Fenchurch Street, St Mary Axe and Duke's Place. They met for secret services in a house in Creechurch Lane with a carefully guarded entrance.

Puritanism represented a return to the Bible and a more approving climate was emerging for a possible return of the Jews to England. Some Puritans relished the hope that if they did they would be unable to withstand the attraction of the Puritan brand of Christianity and would become genuine converts.

Menasseh ben Israel and his petition

Rabbi Menasseh ben Israel (1604–57), who was well aware of the growing pro-Jewish sentiment in England, was living in Amsterdam. Fluent in several European languages and in Latin, he was widely respected for his secular and

Menasseh ben Israel. He petitioned Oliver Cromwell to allow the Jews to return to England. (From an etching by Rembrandt.)

religious knowledge. He was highly thought of in the Christian as well as the Jewish world and many Gentiles flocked to hear him preach.

He subscribed to the theory that the Jews needed to return to England because, according to the Scriptures (Daniel 7:7 and Deuteronomy 28:64), Jews had to be scattered to all corners of the world before the Messiah would come.

Jews, it was reported, had recently been discovered in America and their presence was missing only in England. If they returned to England, Menasseh and his followers believed, the Messianic Deliverance could begin.

Menasseh had met many Puritans in Amsterdam, and as a result of conversations with them was emboldened to approach Cromwell. He arrived in London in 1655 with a formal petition seeking permission for Jews to return to England, for free exercise of their religion, the right to establish synagogues and cemeteries, and the right to trade. At the same time it was agreed that all those who were admitted should swear allegiance to the Government. Cromwell convened a conference in the Council Chamber in Whitehall attended by leading theologians, parliamentarians, diplomats, lawyers and merchants. They met on five days in December to consider two questions: was it lawful for the Jews to return and, if so, on what terms?

The first question was quickly decided in favour of the Jews. The lawyers ruled that the expulsion had simply been by royal decree and that there was no statute or other legality barring their re-entry. But on the second point there was considerable disagreement. Some of the clergy regarded the public exercise of the Jewish religion as blasphemous; others feared that the Jews might try to convert Christians to Judaism. Rumours were spread that the Jews had offered half a million pounds for St Paul's Cathedral for use as a synagogue. The merchants were totally against the idea, fearing competition, and argued that admitting the Jews would cause the decline of English trade.

Cromwell sensed that the conference was not going to recommend an unqualified return of the Jews so he dismissed it and said that the Government would reflect on what had been said during the debates and make a decision. In fact, no formal statement was delivered, but Cromwell quietly acquiesced to the return of the Jews: those already in England, and others who decided to come, were allowed to stay. The Jews had not been recalled, but their presence was henceforth considered legitimate. It was to Carvajal that Cromwell gave the assurance of the right of Jews to remain in England.

The Marranos threw off their masks, and others openly joined them. Menasseh ben Israel returned to Amsterdam and died the next year, aged 53, a

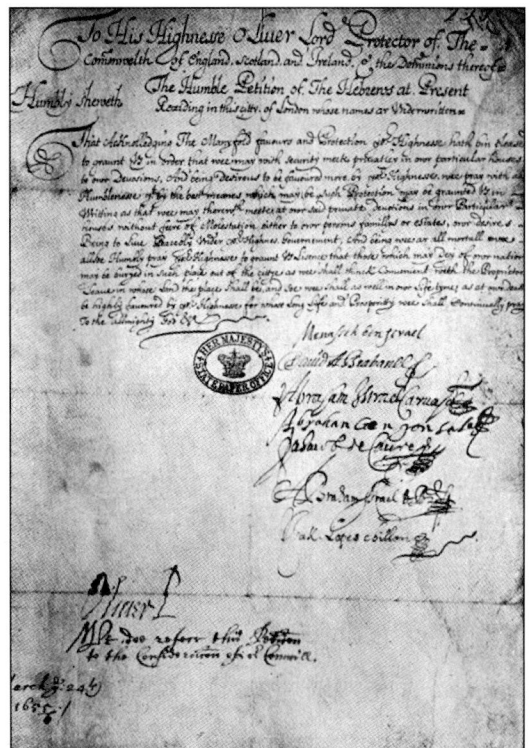

Menasseh ben Israel's petition. He requested that the Jews be allowed free exercise of their religion, the right to establish synagogues and cemeteries, and the right to trade.

The petition was considered in the Council Chamber in Whitehall over five days in December 1655 by leading theologians, parliamentarians, diplomats, lawyers and merchants.

disappointed man because he had not obtained a statutory right of entry. He was being too hard on himself, for he had undoubtedly laid the foundation for future Jewish communities in London and throughout England. From then on, with only a few setbacks, the community grew in numbers and freedoms. Cromwell was proved right: the first Jewish settlers brought money and trade for the benefit of the country.

Chapter 3

1656–1700: Re-admission

The Sephardim and the Ashkenazim

The London community slowly expanded. The first arrivals were, like the Marranos, Sephardim; that is Jews of Mediterranean and Middle Eastern origin. They came to England largely from Spain and Portugal, but also from the Canary Islands, Amsterdam, Hamburg, Leghorn and the south of France, to which they had previously emigrated. This time the newcomers took up residence not in Old Jewry but in the area of Houndsditch, Duke's Place, Petticoat Lane (then called Hog Street) and Jewry Street, all on the edge of the City. They set about establishing the community's essential institutions: a synagogue, a cemetery and a school.

A small synagogue that was opened in Creechurch Lane in 1657 fortunately escaped damage in the Great Fire of 1666, and became one of the sights of London, a fashionable place to visit. One John Greenhalgh, who was invited to the synagogue by 'a learned Jew with a mighty bush', reported in 1662 that there were about 100 in the congregation, all men, most of them 'richly clad'. He was impressed that each child present was able to read the Hebrew texts.

When Samuel Pepys attended on 14 October 1663 he noted approvingly that at the end of the service there was a prayer for the king, 'in which they pronounced his name in Portuguese … but Lord! To see the disorder, laughing, sporting and not attention but confusion in all their service … would make a man forswear ever seeing them more'. By pure chance, he had visited on *Simchat Torah*, a joyous festival celebrating the conclusion of the annual reading of the Torah. It is the one day of the year on which Jews are allowed to dance and sing exuberantly during the service, a day on which the adults may indulge in generous drinking of alcohol, and the children play practical jokes on their seniors. It is not surprising that Pepys was shocked. Eventually, so great was the stream of Gentile visitors that it distracted the worshippers, and an end had to be put to the practice. The synagogue was extended in 1673 to seat 174 men and 84 women.

Grounds for a cemetery were purchased in the Mile End Road, then outside the furthest limits of the East End. The friendly relationship between the local church authorities and their Jewish parishioners was well illustrated by the tolling of church bells on the occasion of Jewish funerals. Among the first burials were 21 victims of the Great Plague of 1665.

When Charles II came to the throne, City merchants were still fearful of competition from the newcomers, and they made further attempts to restrict their activity. Their efforts failed because both Charles and his brother and successor James II were prepared to protect the community. While Charles was in exile in Holland, Jews there helped him financially and he promised to protect them if he was restored to the throne. He kept his word, and the attempt was defeated. On 22 August 1664 the Privy Council declared that the Jews could expect 'the same favour as formerly they had so long as they lived peaceably with due obedience to his Majesty's law and without scandal to his government'. This was the first written statement that Jewish residence in England was not to be disturbed. The queen, Catherine of Braganza, who married Charles in 1662, brought a Jewish physician with her, Dr Fernando Mendez. Also in her entourage were the brothers Duarte and Francisca da Sylva, Portuguese-born Jewish bankers of Amsterdam, to whom she entrusted the management of her dowry.

In 1664, the Gates of Hope, a boys' school for poor Jewish children, was founded and supported out of synagogue funds. Originally confined to religious and Hebrew studies, arithmetic and the reading and writing of English were later added. The school regulations required every boy to arrive at school cleanly washed and combed. His feet had to be washed once in every week, and his hair cut once in every month at least. It was not until 1730 that the Villa Real, a similar school for educating 'the daughters of the poor members of the synagogue', was opened.

In 1679 the community started an event that lasted a century, the presentation of an annual gift, usually silver plate, to the Lord Mayor of London. Samples of these gifts can be found on display in the Jewish Museum in Albert Street, Camden Town.

When William of Orange planned to come to England, he was held up by lack of money. His invasion was financed by Lopes Suaso, who told him 'if you are fortunate I know you will pay me back. If you are unlucky, I agree to lose my money.' Once William was safely installed he encouraged several Jewish financiers, led by Isaac Pereiro who became Commissary General, to move to London.

In the meantime immigrant Ashkenazim, Jews of central and eastern European origin, were slowly growing in numbers. Whereas the Sephardim included merchants, commodity brokers, dealers in precious stones and jewellery and several physicians, the Ashkenazim in the main were poorer. The majority of their early arrivals were unskilled and without capital, and they turned their hand to minor commerce – street trading, itinerant peddling, selling old clothes and small-scale shopkeeping.

Their most prominent member was Benjamin Levy, who had arrived in about 1669. The son of a wealthy Hamburg merchant, he was one of the 12 Jews out of 124 men licensed to practise as a broker on the Royal Exchange, and was one of the original subscribers to the Bank of England.

The Ashkenazim met in a private home for prayer meetings, but by 1690 they were numerous enough to warrant the building of a synagogue of their own. This was erected in Duke's Place, Aldgate, and was paid for by Levy. They formed their own burial society (*Chevra Kadisha*) and for £190 acquired a piece of land on a 999-year lease for use as a cemetery, adjoining that of the Sephardim. Its entrance is now in Alderney Road. Levy, his second wife and some of the founders of the Ashkenazi community are buried there.

The Ashkenazi community's first charity, *Bikkur Cholim*, the Society for Visiting the Sick and Burying the Dead, was established in 1664. A communal physician was appointed at a salary of £10 per annum to attend to the poor, an office that continued until 1948.

As the century came to a close, there were around 1,000 Jews in London, half of whom depended on charitable relief from the community.

Chapter 4

1700–1800: Consolidation and Growth

THE start of the 18th century marked the beginning of growth for the Jewish community and a greater acceptance of its position within wider society. A knighthood granted in 1700 to the financier Solomon de Medina, the Army contractor to William III and the first professing Jew to be so honoured, was a significant landmark, indicating just how far the contribution made by Jews to the well-being of the nation had been recognised and how integrated the community had already become.

A steady stream, averaging about 200 a year, continued to arrive from Holland, Poland and Germany. Events that triggered further Jewish immigration into London included the intensification of the Portuguese Inquisition in the 1720s and 1730s, a wave of new massacres in Eastern Europe in 1768, the problems created for the Jews during the events leading to the partition of Poland in 1772, and the siege of Gibraltar, which had a large Jewish presence, in the 1780s. Over the course of the 100 years from 1700 the number of Jews in England and Wales rose from just 1,000 to about 20,000. By this time the gener-

Interior of Bevis Marks, c.1884 (By courtesy of the Guildhall Library, Corporation of London)

al population was some nine million, so the Jews still accounted for less than half of one per cent of the total.

The immigrants who came to England had chosen wisely, for Jews in Georgian England enjoyed a greater degree of social acceptance and religious tolerance than anywhere else in continental Europe. Even in Holland they were excluded from certain towns and cities. In Germany and Italy the ghetto system still prevailed, and there was complete exclusion from Spain and Portugal.

In England, by contrast, they were under the protection of the law, could settle anywhere, and enjoyed virtual, if not quite complete, social equality. The disabilities from which they undoubtedly suffered in public life – being excluded from any office under the Crown, any part in civic government, or any employment, however modest, connected with the administration of justice or education – were restrictions held in common with other nonconformist groups. It was obligatory on all persons seeking such appointments to take the Sacrament in accordance with the rites of the Church of England, and that excluded Roman Catholics and other non-Anglicans, not Jews alone.

Of course, anti-Semitic sentiment still existed within society, and there were some setbacks. A child ritual murder story went the rounds in 1732 and Jews were attacked in the streets of London until the story was proved false when

Scene in the Great Synagogue before the reading of the Law. Early 19th century.

Interior view of the New Synagogue, c.1911, taken at the time of the Festival of Shavuot when the synagogue is decorated with plants and flowers. (By courtesy of the Guildhall Library, Corporation of London)

Entrance to Duke's Place, from an engraving dating from 1790.

the true offender was arrested. In 1744 a bequest of £1,000 for the maintenance of a Talmudical college (a seminary of advanced Jewish scholarship) in London was declared illegal by the courts on the grounds that such a college would be a superstitious institution. The money was passed to the Foundling Hospital in Coram Fields to support a teacher to instruct the children there in the Christian religion.

However apart from one or two isolated incidents, during which no deaths occurred, there were no violent manifestations of anti-Semitism, not even during the outcry over the Jew Bill that will be discussed later.

The London Synagogues during the 18th century

The synagogue obviously plays an important part in Jewish life. Membership rates have always been comparatively high, even among the non-observant who become members because they feel the need to have an attachment to the community and desire to be buried as Jews.

In 1701, the Sephardi community opened a new synagogue in Bevis Marks, just a stone's throw from Creechurch Lane. It was basically a copy of the Amsterdam synagogue. Some of the seats from the original synagogue in Creechurch Lane were moved to the new synagogue and are still there today. The builder was a Quaker named Avis who, it was said, when handing over the synagogue repaid his profit to the members, saying that he could not make a gain out of the erection of a House of God.

In the centre are seven hanging many-branched candelabra, representing the seven days of the week, one sent by the Amsterdam synagogue, and still used to light the synagogue with candlelight on festival days after dark. There are 10 brass candlesticks symbolising the Ten Commandments, and 12 columns supporting the gallery signifying the Twelve Tribes of Israel. Princess Anne, later Queen Anne, presented an oak beam from one of the Royal Navy's ships that was incorporated in the roof of the building. Apart from some roof works carried out in 1738, and bomb damage caused during an IRA attack in

1992, the synagogue remains unchanged today. Services are regularly held, and visits can be made by prior appointment.

The Sephardim remained united, but the Ashkenazim exhibited a more common feature of Jewish religious life, schism. The saying 'two Jews three opinions' is not without some basis in fact. There is scarcely a synagogue in the world of any great age that can boast a history that does not at least once involve a breakaway group leaving over some grievance, real or imagined, about ritual, or the honorary officers, or the allocation of seats. The story that a Jew stranded on a desert island built himself two synagogues, the second being the one he would not be seen dead in, is not too fanciful to be true.

A group, led by a prosperous gem dealer, Marcus Moses, broke away from the Duke's Place community in 1706 over a matter of interpretation of Jewish law. Initially services were held in his house in Magpie Alley, Fenchurch Street, and later, in 1725, a fine synagogue, known as the Hambro, was erected in the garden of the house and remained there until 1892. Moses also, in 1707, purchased a burial ground at Hoxton on a 150-year lease at 10 shillings per annum for the congregation. It contains the graves of the Hamburger, Gompertz, Amschel and Salomons families. In 1899 a new Hambro synagogue was consecrated in Adler Street, Whitechapel (named after Chief Rabbi Hermann Adler), but that closed in 1936 and amalgamated with the Great Synagogue.

In 1722, the Ashkenazim replaced their synagogue in Duke's Place with a

Interior of the Hambro Synagogue, Fenchurch Street, founded in 1725.

much more substantial building costing £2,000. It was paid for by Moses Hart, a broker and government agent in stocks. It was money he could well afford, for in addition to his success in business he had married a wealthy wife and was the winner of £20,000 in the national lottery. The synagogue, which came to be known as the Great Synagogue, remained the main Ashkenazi synagogue until it was destroyed by Hitler's bombs in 1941.

The synagogue was famous for its musical services and one member of the choir, Myer Lyon, whose stage name was Leoni, achieved such fame that he attracted overflowing congregations that included many Christians. The Revd Charles Wesley was so impressed and moved by his rendering of *Yigdal*, a hymn based on Maimonides' *Thirteen Principles of Faith,* that he arranged for it to be adapted as a Wesleyan hymn, *The God of Abraham Praise,* that sold thousands of copies.

Decorum, often a problem in synagogues, was efficiently maintained. Under threat of fines the congregation were enjoined not to chew tobacco in the synagogue, not to attend service wearing slippers ('unless he has sore feet') or caps. In 1755 ladies were banned from wearing crinoline hoops on the High Holy days when the synagogue was particularly crowded since their costume occupied fully three times as much cubic space as the female body.

When the Great Synagogue was totally rebuilt in 1790 to provide accommodation for 500 men and 250 women, its main benefactor was Mrs Judith Levy, a daughter of Moses Hart and the wife of a prominent merchant engaged in the Lisbon diamond trade. She had an acute business sense, and not only aided her husband in his business but successfully invested in shares on her own account and increased her already handsome fortune. After her husband's death in 1750 she bought No.4, Maids-of-Honour Row in Richmond, where she lived during her long widowhood, entertaining lavishly, making large charitable donations, but eventually becoming increasingly eccentric. She became known as the 'Queen of Richmond Green'.

A third East End synagogue, the New Synagogue, opened in 1761 in Bricklayers' Hall in Leadenhall Street. In 1837, it moved to Great St Helen's and then, in 1915, to Egerton Road, Stamford Hill. The community thus had four important synagogues in the East End by 1800: Bevis Marks, the Great, the Hambro and the New.

Judith Levy (1706–1803) paid for the rebuilding of the Great Synagogue in 1790. She lived at No.4 Maids-of-Honour Row in Richmond and was known as the Queen of Richmond Green.

In the meantime, more and more Jews came to live in the West End of London. By the mid-18th century the rate books showed there were several Jewish families in and around Rupert Street, Broadwick Street, Berwick Street, Carnaby Street, Great Windmill Street, Leicester Square, the Strand, Pulteney Street, Panton Street and Orange Street – enough to justify holding regular services.

From about 1761 these were held in the house of Wolf Liepman, a philanthropic patron of learning and culture, in Great Pulteney Street. Thus was born *Hebra Kaddisha Shel Gemilluth Hassadim Westminster*, later known as the Western Synagogue. It became a combination of synagogue and burial society, with some features of a friendly society. The *minyan* moved first to a hired room in Back Alley, Denmark Court, in the Strand, on the site of the present Strand Palace Hotel, and then in 1797 to Dibdin's Theatre, Sans Souci, also in Denmark Court. The latter building had previously been occupied as a picture gallery by the Royal Academy, and boasted a hall of some 50 feet by 36 feet, as well as two rooms for vestry and office purposes.

Entrance to the New Synagogue, Leadenhall Street, c.1762

The Strand and certain other streets nearby were infamous for their houses of ill-repute, but by the synagogue's rules any person keeping a disorderly house was debarred from all religious privileges.

The congregation included Jewish coachmen and footmen, butlers and valets who waited upon their blue-blooded masters in the Sephardi community as well as upon non-Jewish nobility and gentry. Silken breeches and golden hose were not regarded as an enhancement of the dignity of a house of worship, and a rule was introduced that 'no flunkey in livery' could have an *aliya,* that is be called up to participate in the reading of the Torah.

The Parish Overseer annotated the rate books – 'Denmark Court, as respectable as most of the courts in this ward. Here the Christian and the Jew associate in apparent harmony, an instructive example to the rest of the community.' There never came a time when it needed to be said that this harmony no longer prevailed. Overt anti-Semitism only infrequently reared its head in the West End.

In 1810, the almost inevitable occurred: there was an internal squabble of which the cause was obscure. A breakaway movement, calling itself 'The Pillars of Uprightness', established a rival congregation. Its leaders hired a room for services first in Dean Street, a little later in Brewer Street, and finally in larger premises in Maiden Lane, Covent Garden. It became known as the Maiden Lane Synagogue and purchased its own burial ground in Bancroft Road, Mile End. It did not rejoin the main congregation until almost 100 years later in 1907.

The Western subsequently moved to St Alban's Place in the Haymarket in 1826, then in 1874 to Alfred Place off Tottenham Court Road, where it remained until destroyed by bombing in April 1941. It moved from there to Crawford Street in Marylebone, and finally in 1991 amalgamated with the Marble Arch Synagogue in Great Cumberland Place under the title of the Western Marble Arch.

The Chief Rabbinate

When, in 1765, David Schiff was appointed rabbi of the Great Synagogue, he assumed the title of 'Rabbi of London and the Provinces'. Rabbi Meshullum Solomon, the rabbi of the Hambro, did likewise. There was some disagreement as to which of them was right; some favoured Schiff, others favoured Solomon. It was not until 1802, when Rabbi Solomon Hirschell was appointed by the Great Synagogue, that the matter was resolved. He became accepted and recognised as the Chief Rabbi by the other London synagogues, the provincial synagogues, and later by the colonial synagogues.

Each Chief Rabbi has been long-serving. In the past 200 years there have been just seven: Solomon Hirschell 1802–42; Nathan Marcus Adler 1845–90; his son, Hermann Adler, 1890–1911; Joseph Herman Hertz 1913–46; Israel Brodie 1948–65; Immanuel Jakobovits 1967–91; and the present incumbent Jonathan Sacks, whose official designation is Chief Rabbi of the United Hebrew Congregation of the Commonwealth, although not all sections of the community recognise his authority or accept that he can speak on behalf of Anglo-Jewry generally.

Solomon Hirschell (1762–1842) was rabbi of the Great Synagogue from 1802–42 and was recognised as the first Chief Rabbi of England.

The Jew Bill of 1753

Under Cromwell only a few Jews had been naturalised, but Charles II and James II were more liberal in this regard, and during their reigns most of the leaders of the community became English citizens.

However, unnaturalised foreign-born Jews laboured under the disadvantage that they could not own land or ships. Following an approach from the Sephardi community to the Government a Bill was introduced into the House of Lords in April 1753 providing simply that Jews who had been resident in Great Britain or Ireland for three years or more might, as Christian aliens could, be naturalised on application to Parliament without taking the Sacrament. Both the Jews and the Government believed that the climate of opinion was sufficiently favourable for this change. They were proved wrong. Though the Bill passed easily though the House of Lords, opposition began to develop during the second reading in the House of Commons. Petitions against the Bill flooded in, particularly from merchants who had faced Jewish competition, and from others who claimed that the Bill would dishonour the Christian religion. Despite this the Bill received the royal assent and passed into law.

The opposition then transferred from Parliament to the streets, and agitation against the 'Jew Bill' sprang up throughout the country. An election was looming, and candidates, seeing an opportunity to acquire popularity among the electorate, outbid each other with their calls to repeal the Act. Posters plastered the walls alleging that ministers had been corrupted by bribes of half a million pounds, and the slogan 'Christianity and Old England for Ever' was heard everywhere. The printing houses daily turned out pamphlets, ballads and caricatures denouncing the Bill and all the old anti-Semitic libels were revived and recirculated, including the fable of ritual murder. It was alleged that there would be an influx of foreign Jews who would divide England among their tribes as their ancestors had done in the land of Canaan. One satirist suggested that the importing of pork would be forbidden and Christmas would be abolished.

Some clergymen and newspapers gave a more balanced view and emphasised the economic benefits that the Jews had brought, and would bring, should they be persuaded to settle in greater numbers. They pointed out that the Jews' practice of supporting their own poor would mean there would be no burden on the public purse. But bishops who had supported the Bill were booed when they appeared in public. The Archbishop of Canterbury, who was kindly disposed towards the Jews, feared that in the rising heated atmosphere massacres might follow. He said, 'we are now treating the Jews just as the Mohammedans treat the Christians'.

So intense and widespread was the outcry that the Government was compelled to bow to the pressure. The imminence of the general election was a deciding factor, and the Duke of Newcastle, the government leader in the House of Lords, introduced a measure of repeal in Parliament. It received the royal assent in December 1753. It was perhaps the shortest-lived piece of legislation ever. It was not until 90 years later that the long struggle for the natural-isation of foreign Jews was brought to a success-ful conclusion. The deep disappointment gener-ated by the repeal faded within a short time. Some Jews determined to own land or ships converted to Christianity.

While aliens were always regarded with a certain amount of suspicion, they could nonethe-less prosper. Eighteenth-century England was a country open to entrepreneuri-al talent, and offered scope for initiative and enterprise. She had opened new worlds of commerce in the Americas, the West Indies and the East, and the constant movement of large armies and vast fleets offered great opportunities to merchants, especially for those, like the Jews, who had international connections.

One of the most remarkable and influential men of his time was Samson Gideon (1699–1762). He was shrewd, pleasant and witty, and a descendant of a Lisbon family that had produced great scientists and poets. His father, an active member of Bevis Marks, had amassed a fortune in West India trade and came to London in 1680. Samson started with an initial capital of £1,500 and began business as a dealer in lottery tickets. In 1729, he became one of the 12 permitted Jewish brokers on the Exchange, an appointment he held until 1752. He carried on business in Ludgate Street and from 1749 in his large house in Lincoln's Inn Fields. From the very first he showed himself to be a man of the highest integrity and honour and he rose to become one of the most promi-nent financiers in the City, where he was known as the 'Great Oracle' of the stock markets and the 'Pillar of State Credit'.

Aaron Hart (1670–1756) was rabbi of the Great Synagogue from 1704–56.

The South Sea Bubble, the greatest financial scandal in history, led to massive bankruptcies. Very few Jewish financiers had invested, believing that if something looked too good to be true it probably was.

In 1720, the South Sea Bubble burst – the greatest financial scandal in history – a fraud that had entangled royalty, politicians, the professional classes, gamblers and con-men, all seeking untold riches by frenzied investment in worthless companies. George I gave Sir Robert Walpole, England's first Prime Minister, the task of helping to restore the badly shaken confidence of the City and the public at large. Walpole in turn called upon Gideon, and was fortunate to have at his side a man who had stood firm when the crash occurred, and who when everybody was gambling had not been carried away by the fevered speculation. Other Jewish financiers had similarly remained aloof from the mania that developed, believing that if something looked too good to be true it probably was. After the crash, when insolvencies rose to an alarming height, few Jewish names were to be found in the list of bankruptcies. Gideon devised a scheme for raising £3 million pounds for the Government, making himself answerable for a considerable part of it, and the market steadied. It saved the day.

Things looked even worse in 1745 when Charles Edward Stuart, 'Bonnie Prince Charlie' the Young Pretender, and his Jacobite rebel army approached

Plan of the two Mile End cemeteries in 1786.

London. Government stocks fell disastrously in value. George II collapsed under the strain, and Pelham, the Prime Minister, was undecided what to do. The Jews rose splendidly to the occasion – they enlisted in the militia in great numbers, aroused confidence by accepting bank notes at their full value, and imported gold into England. In that period fraught with danger, Samson Gideon not only succeeded in raising a loan of £1.7 million, but to support the credit of the state he bought into the market with all the ready cash at his disposal, and in order to buy more pledged his name and reputation. Financial disaster was again averted.

From then on Gideon was permanent adviser to the Government in financial matters and devoted almost the whole of his time to the public service for which he neither asked nor received any fee or commission.

Gideon had married a Protestant and their children were all baptised at St Paul's Cathedral. Though he had fallen out with his synagogue, Bevis Marks, in 1753, and instructed them no longer to consider him a member, he anonymously continued his subscriptions. His will included a legacy of £1,000 to the synagogue to cover his burial at the Mile End Cemetery and a request that his name should be recalled with those of other benefactors during the annual recital of prayers for the dead made on the Day of Atonement. He had sought the best of both worlds; he wanted to enjoy the status and life of an English country gentleman without forfeiting his soul; to live like a Christian and die as a Jew. To an extent he succeeded.

Perhaps the most significant event of all during these early days was the establishment in 1732 of a Talmud Torah within the Great Synagogue. This was the origin of the Jews' Free School that became a most important influence on future generations of immigrant Jews. It is a subject to which we shall return.

Occupations

The range of occupations of the Jewish poor began to expand. The majority were still engaged in petty trades as peddlers and hawkers, orange sellers and old clothes men, but Jewish masters employing apprentices between 1710 and 1773 included wigmakers, diamond polishers, shipwrights, booksellers, cobblers, engravers, pencil makers, watchmakers, butchers, barbers and stationers. Gradually, more of a lower middle-class community was emerging.

The Jewish 'ole-clothes man' was still a common sight. In the days before cheap tailoring, labourers had to be content with cast-off clothing. Every street, lane and alley in London was patrolled by itinerant Jewish hawkers, many long-bearded and speaking a fractured English, prepared to buy second-hand clothing as well as every other conceivable discarded household article. Clothing was 'clobbered', that is renovated, by Jewish needlewomen and sold in Rag Fair, a market situated in Rosemary Lane (later renamed Royal Mint Street) near the Tower of London. Clothing past redemption was sold as rags.

Professional sport has always been an important avenue of upward social mobility for the poor, and a way of gaining popular recognition not only for oneself but also for the group to which one belongs. The classic modern example is Mohammed Ali, formerly Cassius Clay; Daniel Mendoza, a descendant of Spanish Marranos, was Anglo-Jewry's Mohammed Ali.

Born in 1764 and living in Bethnal Green, he often got involved in fights in his youth as he defended fellow Jews from the insults and threats of their non-Jewish neighbours. His first professional fight was in Mile End in 1784, when he beat Harry the Coalheaver in 40 rounds, a bout that lasted almost two hours. Though short and light and having to take on opponents who were taller and heavier, he went on to become British champion. He achieved this by using a more scientific approach to boxing, replacing the brutal slugging of the day with clever footwork and defence. He always insisted on being billed as 'Mendoza the Jew' and made boxing socially acceptable. He enjoyed the patronage of the Prince of Wales, later to become King George IV, and Lord Byron became an admirer and a pupil when Mendoza set up a boxing academy in Bond Street. Mendoza, hailed as a British hero, and other successful Jewish boxers such as Samuel Elias, said to have invented the uppercut, and the Belasco brothers, countered the stereotype of the Jew and enhanced the reputation and standing of Anglo-Jewry considerably.

Daniel Mendoza (1764–1836) was Anglo-Jewry's Cassius Clay. Boxing champion of England, and hailed as a British hero, he raised the standing of the Jewish community.

The Board of Deputies

On the accession of George III in 1760 the Sephardim, following their long-established custom, sent a loyal deputation to the king who accepted their address kindly. But by now they constituted only about a quarter of the Jewish population and the Ashkenazim were upset by what had happened. It was agreed that in future representatives of both sections of the community would meet to deal with all important public matters affecting the Jews. From this developed the London Committee of Deputies of British Jews, today better known simply as the Board of Deputies.

Until the 1830s it was a somewhat somnolent body, and the holding of meetings only every five or six years was not uncommon. The Board monitored legislation and other matters of government that might affect the community. It came to be recognised as an official institutional body of Anglo-Jewry in the early 19th century, and has since been accepted as such.

At first membership was composed exclusively of representatives of orthodox synagogues, but today all properly constituted synagogues and other significant communal organisations have seats on the Board. It collects statistical and demographic information, undertakes research on and for the community, maintains contact with and provides support for Jewish communities around the world, and acts as a public relations vehicle for promoting the Jewish viewpoint and fighting anti-Semitism. The Board elected its first female President in 2000, Mrs Jo Wagerman, a former head teacher of the Jews' Free School. She recently retired due to ill-health.

Charitable Institutions

The East End has always been a home of good causes; it had ragged schools, philanthropic societies, free dispensaries, relief societies, orphanages (Dr Barnado was the son of a Sephardi Jew who could trace his family ancestry back in a direct line for 350 years) and societies for improving the condition of the working classes.

As the Jewish community grew so it enlarged its own charities. Those started by the Sephardim in the 18th century included societies providing lying-in facilities (1724), dowers (1736), loans (1749), food and groceries (1775) and apprenticeships. It had a home for the sick and aged, the *Beth Holim*, which opened in Leman Street in 1748 and later moved to the Mile End Road.

Not to be outdone, the Ashkenazim provided a charity for assisting the poor with food and other Sabbath necessities and weekly provisions in winter, a physician to look after its poor, a home for the aged, *Neveh Zedek*, and a bread, meat and coal society whose first president, in 1780, was Levi Barent Cohen (1740–1808). He had settled in London from Amsterdam in 1770 and later became the father-in-law of both Sir Moses Montefiore and Nathan Mayer Rothschild.

Alongside the synagogue-inspired bodies there were numerous voluntary associations – mutual help societies, burial societies, societies for visiting the sick, educating the young and relieving imprisoned debtors. From the mid-18th-century friendly societies on the English model began to make their appearance.

The basic objective of the Jewish charities, whether synagogal or communal, was to put the poor in the position where they could look after themselves rather than simply meet their immediate need. They equipped them with a small capital or stock-in-trade and sent them out to earn a living in the only callings that the intolerances of the time left fully open to them: hawking, peddling and old clothes dealing. Those thus engaged formed the bulk of the communal proletariat, painfully gaining their livelihood, consolidating their positions, and ultimately becoming self-supporting.

Education

Where the community leaders had scandously failed in their duty was in the provision they had made for educating the children of the poor. The Gates of Hope, the Villa Real and the Talmud Torah of the Great Synagogue catered for very few pupils. In contrast, the Church of England and the nonconformists each had strong educational bodies, the National Society and the British and Foreign Society respectively, and both opened free schools within easy reach of the Jewish community. The National made no concessions to its Jewish pupils, and even the British and Foreign decided that the Jewish claim for exemption from lessons on the New Testament could not be granted, although 'every care would be taken to avoid wounding the feelings of parents and children'.

Increasing numbers of Jewish children attended these schools, and though they did not have conversion in mind, there was great concern that Jewish children were inevitably becoming subject to Christian influence and at risk of losing their heritage; that they might be saturated with Christianity without being conscious of it. The view was expressed that:

> The blank leaf between the Old and New Testament in our Bibles may thus be turned, so gradually, so slyly, as not even to be noticed by the most wary parents. Specific Jewish schools are therefore preferable for Jewish children where communities are large enough and wealthy enough to support such institutions of their own.

Patrick Colquhoun, the London magistrate. In 1796 he castigated the Ashkenazi community for not providing adequate schooling for the children of their poor. (By courtesy of the Guildhall Library, Corporation of London)

One of the fine houses in Mansell Street of the type occupied by successful businessmen, c.1886. (By courtesy of the Guildhall Library, Corporation of London)

Action was called for but nothing effective was done, and to exacerbate the situation Jewish youth were implicated in the crime wave that swept through England in the fourth quarter of the 18th century. This led to public criticism by Patrick Colquhoun, a liberal-minded London magistrate and sociologist.

In 1796 Colquhoun published *A Treatise on the Police of the Metropolis*, in which he gave an account of the pitiable and shocking conditions of the poor in London, 'containing detail of the VARIOUS CRIMES AND MISDEMEANORS by which Public and Private Property are, at present, injured and endangered; and SUGGESTING REMEDIES for their PREVENTION'. He identified drunkenness as the most prominent cause of crime. Jews rarely frequented the ale houses that were 'the receptacles of idleness and vice', and were free of many crimes he mentioned, but he nonetheless had harsh criticism to make of the community.

The Jews had their fair share of vagrants, beggars, the destitute, the unemployed, and homeless boys and girls roaming the streets. Colquhoun said that 'most of the lower classes of those distinguished by the name of German or Dutch Jews, [that is the Ashkenazim], live chiefly by their wits, and establish a system of mischievous intercourse all over the country, the better to carry on their fraudulent designs'. He exempted the Sephardim from his strictures. They, he said, were generally opulent and respectable, and gave their children the best education that could be obtained, but the children of the Ashkenazim:

very seldom trained to any trade or occupation by which they can earn their livelihood by manual labour: their youths excluded from becoming apprentices, and their females from hiring themselves generally as

servants, on account of the superstitious adherence to their ceremoni-
al traditions … nothing can exceed their melancholy condition, both
with regard to themselves and Society. Thus excluded from these
resources, which other classes of the Community possess, they seem to
have no alternative but to resort to tricks and devices to enable them
… to live in idleness. The habits they thus acquire are of the most
mischievous and noxious to the Community that can be conceived.

He urged the Sephardim to help the Ashkenazim.

Colquhoun's book was popular, and passed through
several editions. His public strictures could not be ignored.
Joshua Van Oven (1766–1838), a pioneer communal
worker, honorary physician to the Great Synagogue and a
Governor of the Talmud Torah, put himself forward as the
community spokesman, and entered into a dialogue with
Colquhoun. He pointed out that there was still considerable prejudice against Jews. Despite tolerant government,
prejudice was prevalent 'even here', and the Jewish
community had to provide for itself. He claimed it had
done this successfully while their numbers were small, but
the community's wealth had not kept pace with the
increase in the Jewish population in the previous 50 years.
'The opulent are but few, and the middling class although
not so few, possess but little, and the bulk of the Nation
consists of a very numerous poor'. Synagogue funds, he said, were inadequate
to meet the need.

He contended that the Jewish poor were not an idle people, that they
wanted to work, but that there still existed insurmountable obstacles to their
doing so, because legislation barred them from many trades and callings. It was
almost impossible for an observant Jewish child to obtain an apprenticeship
with a Christian master, who could not afford to give time off for the Jewish
Sabbath which reduced the apprentice's working week to four and a half days.
There was, Van Oven said, no circumstance in life more distressing to a Jewish
father (of whatever rank in society) than not being able to put his son forward
in life in some honest industrious occupation.

Van Oven drew up a startlingly ambitious scheme to regulate the Jewish
poor. It called for the establishment of a Jewish Poor Relief Board, to be invested by Parliament with quasi-governmental powers. The Board was to be

Joshua van Oven
(1766–1838), surgeon
to the Great Synagogue
and active in commu-
nal affairs.

allowed to appropriate a certain percentage of the poor rates that Jews paid to the parishes in which they lived, or to tax all Jews directly for the maintenance of their poor. The funds raised in this manner, along with the amounts already distributed by the synagogues, were to be distributed by the Board, which would assume responsibility for the relief of all the Jewish poor in London. Institutional centres would be set up: a workhouse, a hospital for the sick, an asylum for the aged and infirm, and a school to educate children in a trade, 'the whole arranged on a strict Judaic plan with respect to prayers, education, and diet'. Colquhoun approved the scheme, but it required parliamentary approval for which an intermediary with the right contacts was needed. Van Oven knew just the man – a fellow Governor at the Talmud Torah, Abraham Goldsmid.

Abraham and his brother Benjamin were money brokers engaged in government business, whose annual transactions amounted to millions. They enjoyed the friendship of government ministers and even of George III. They were unquestionably philanthropic, and generous to both Jewish and non-Jewish charities. Abraham founded the Royal Naval Asylum. (Despite their apparent worldly success, both later committed suicide after running into financial difficulties.)

Abraham Goldsmid was an ideal choice. He had for some time been struck by the need to provide facilities for the Ashkenazi poor similar to those provided by the Sephardim. With this in view, in 1795 he sent out an appeal for establishing a Jews' Hospital – an institution that not only tended the sick but also provided a home for the helpless poor and teaching facilities for children to learn honest trades. The fund soon reached the very respectable total of £20,000. However, Goldsmid found it easier to raise funds than to establish the hospital. Differences arose among the subscribers as to the precise application of the money, and the whole scheme was becalmed.

Unfortunately, even with the help of Goldsmid, Van Oven's plan never advanced beyond the first stage of the legislative process. On 22 April 1802, 'the affair was given up'. Four more years were to elapse before use was made of the money. In June 1806 a block of houses was purchased in Mile End for £2,300. The Jews' Hospital (*Neveh Tsedek*, literally 'Abode of Righteousness', *Jeremiah* 31:23) was built. (This is not to be confused with the London Jewish Hospital, built more than a century later.) It had two separate depart-

Title page (1795) of the Constitution and Minutes of the Holy Society of Mercy for the Upbringing of Young Orphans, an early Sephardi charity. (Courtesy The Jewish Historical Society of England)

ments – an old age home and a trade school. Initially, there were just 28 residents: five men, five women, ten boys and eight girls.

Emphasis was placed on practical training. The bulk of the school day – two hours in the morning and two hours in the afternoon – was devoted to teaching skills such as shoemaking, chair making and cabinetmaking. The girls were taught to knit, wash, iron, cook, do needlework and clean house. On leaving, the boys were apprenticed to skilled artisans and the girls went into domestic service, generally in Jewish homes. In 1821, there were 47 boys and 29 girls, the growth of the institution being partly due to the generous support of wealthy Christians. But, like the Talmud Torah of the Great Synagogue, it touched the lives of only a small number of children in relation to the size of the entire Jewish population.

Further problems were caused by an accelerating expansion of Evangelism at the end of the 18th century and the beginning of the 19th. An organised effort was made to convert Jews by direct missionary activity. The missionaries concentrated their efforts on poor Jews; the rich and middle classes were not considered likely fodder. They sought to exploit the then current Jewish social conditions. What could have held out greater promise of success for the missionaries than to open free schools that welcomed Jewish children?

The most important Societies were the Missionary Society (not specifically aimed at the Jews), founded in 1795; the London Missionary Society, effectively a committee of the Missionary Society that was created to work exclusively among the Jews; and the London Society for Promoting Christianity among the Jews (LSPCJ), founded in 1809. Between 1806 and 1813, three missionary schools were established in and around the Jewish East End quarter.

Palestine Place, Bethnal Green, c.1840. A school opened in 1812 by the London Society for the Promotion of Christianity amongst the Jews, its aim was to attract and convert Jewish children. (Courtesy Guildhall Library, Corporation of London)

Though the first school was comparatively unsuccessful, the methods it employed to attract Jewish pupils – tantamount to direct bribery – offering food, clothing and even money, greatly provoked the community, particularly Chief Rabbi Hirschell. On successive Sabbaths he preached sermons in the Great Synagogue warning parents not to send their children to the schools. He proclaimed that any who did so would be considered as having been themselves baptised, and would forfeit all claim to be Jews:

> *Abstract of an exhortation delivered by the Rev. Solomon Hirschel, At the Great Synagogue, Duke's Place, on Saturday, Jan 10, A.M. 5567 [1807]: After a discourse on Jeremiah 11: 18–19.*
>
> *I had occasion on the last holy Sabbath, to forewarn every one of our nation not to send any of their Children to the newly-established Free School, instituted by a society of persons, who are not of our religion; until we had, by a proper investigation, determined if it be completely free from any possible harm to the welfare of our religion ...*
>
> *Now having since been fully convinced that the whole purpose of this seeming kind exertion, is but an inviting snare, a decoying experiment to undermine the props of our religion; and the sole intent of this Institution is, at bottom, only to entice innocent Jewish Children, during their early years, from the observance of the Law of Moses; and to eradicate the religion of their fathers and forefathers.*
>
> *On this account, I feel myself necessitated to caution the Congregation in general, that no one do send, or allow to be sent, any Child, whether male or female, to this, or any such School established by strangers to our religion; nor likewise into any Sunday School of that nature.*
>
> *All such persons, therefore, who do act contrary to this prohibition, whether male or female, will be considered as if they had themselves forsaken their religion, and been baptized; and shall lose all title to the name of Jews, and forfeit all claims on the Congregation both in life and death.*
>
> *Every one who feareth God, is hereby reminded of his duty to warn every one who may be ignorant of these circumstances, and acquaint him thereof, that he may escape the snare laid to entangle him. Thus may we hope to see the days when the name of the only God will be hallowed, and the Lord will be one, and his name one! Amen.*

Abstracts of the sermons were printed in Yiddish and English and distributed throughout the Jewish quarter. A deputation from the Great Synagogue called on the Treasurer of the London Missionary Society to complain about the tactics and aims of the missionaries, but its protest was ignored.

HYMN

TO BE SUNG BY THE JEWISH CHILDREN,

Under the patronage of

The London Society

FOR PROMOTING

Christianity amongst the Jews;

Before

A SERMON,

To be preached

In behalf of that Institution,

AT

SALTERS' HALL MEETING, CANNON STREET,

ON SUNDAY EVENING, SEPTEMBER 22, 1811,

BY THE

REV. S. LOWELL, of BRISTOL.

SERVICE TO BEGIN AT HALF PAST SIX O'CLOCK.

OF all the gifts thine hand bestows,
Thou Giver of all good !
Not heav'n itself a richer knows,
Than my Redeemer's blood.

Faith too, the blood-receiving grace,
From the same hand we gain ;
Else, sweetly as it suits our case,
That gift had been in vain.

Till thou thy teaching pow'r apply,
Our hearts refuse to see,

And weak, as a distemper'd eye,
Shut out the view of thee.

Blind to the merits of thy Son,
What mis'ry we endure !
Yet fly that hand, from which alone,
We could expect a cure.

We praise thee, and would praise thee more,
To thee our all we owe ;
The precious Saviour, and the pow'r
That makes him precious too.

London : Printed for the Society, at their Office, 6, Devonshire Street, by B. R. GOAKMAN.

The London Society for Promoting Christianity amongst the Jews. Poster giving a hymn to be sung at a meeting on 22 September 1811.

The second school, opened by the LSPCJ, was a little more successful. It was housed in a building in Brick Lane, which at the end of the century became the home of the ultra-orthodox *Machzike Hadath*. In its Report, issued in May 1812, the Society claimed that 83 Jewish boys and girls had been admitted. But many of the 'converts' were children of mixed parentage, Jewish and Gentile, who scarcely knew what their religion was. Such evidence as exists shows that a high proportion lapsed, and the cost of each genuine convert was out of all proportion to the monies expended. An anonymous poet, quoted by Professor Todd Endelman in his book *The Jews of Georgian England*, summed up the matter:

> *Tis true 'tis strange, and strange 'tis true,*
> *Cash buys but cannot keep a Jew.*
> *The meanest, trembling, bribed to lie,*
> *Back to the 'God of Israel' fly.*
>
> *All faiths are equal to a wretch in need.*
> *Not one from choice has joined their train,*
> *Or can from principle remain.*
> *Aware of this, they compromise,*
> *And wear a sort of thin disguise.*
>
> *So Cohen can both faiths unite,*
> *Still Jew, and yet a Christian quite;*
> *Receives the rites and pay of both,*
> *And serves two masters nothing loth.*

In 1812, the LSPCJ began work on a school for boys and girls in 'Palestine Place', Bethnal Green, alongside its church. The entrance was through lodge gates in Cambridge Road, opposite where Cambridge Heath Station was subsequently built. Its foundation stone was laid by the Duke of Kent on 7 April 1813, in the presence of nearly 2,000 spectators. This school had slightly greater success, in terms of numbers, in attracting Jewish pupils, but not in keeping them within their fold. (Some time later, His Royal Highness discovered the nature of the methods followed, and withdrew his patronage.) As their efforts faltered, so they altered their tactics. Until 1829, the gospel was *offered* to Jewish children, 'now its blessed offers are to be *pressed* upon the unwilling and reluctant'. The school remained open until almost the end of the century. Charles Booth, in his *Life and Labour of the People in London*, published in 1892, said it then housed 40 Jewish children, 'but the number of converts is infinitesimal and throws an interesting side light on the moral tenacity of the Jewish race'.

Though none of the missionary schools had any significant success, the cumulative effect of their schools and the church schools was too great to be opposed merely with exhortations and deputations. The problem remained unsolved until the community leaders acted decisively. They agreed to enlarge the Talmud Torah of the Great Synagogue and create a school for boys.

Premises were found in Ebenezer Square near Petticoat Lane and registration began on 13 April 1817. On that day, 102 boys enrolled aged from seven upwards and teaching began three days later. It was soon discovered just how strongly the Jewish poor yearned for an education for their children: less than two months later there were 220 pupils, and their number was increasing daily. The building soon proved too small, and there was a growing demand that provision should be made for the education of girls. It was decided to move the school to a larger site, for boys and girls, in Bell Lane, a street leading off Wentworth Street. It opened in 1822.

The demand for places was phenomenal. In 1846 there were 1,150 pupils and in 1856 1,500, by which time it was the largest school in England. In 1865 the roll rose to 2,000, in 1870 to 2,500, by 1883 to 3,500, and at the turn of the 20th century it had no fewer than 4,250 pupils – it was the largest school in the world. The further development and the impact of this remarkable school upon London's Jewry will be discussed later in the book.

Chapter 5

1800–1880: Emancipation

THE new century started literally with a bang. On the evening of 15 May 1800, George III, Queen Charlotte and the royal princesses attended Drury Lane Theatre. As the king was entering the Royal Box to the applause of the audience, a would-be assassin, James Hadfield, who had placed himself in the middle of the front row of the pit, raised his arm and fired a pistol at the king. The shot missed the king's head by just 14 inches because a Jew, David Moses Dyte, struck Hadfield on the arm and deflected his aim. Dyte was rewarded by being given the patent of selling opera tickets, then a monopoly at the royal disposal. He was appointed Purveyor of Pens and Quills to the Royal Household in 1820 and traded at No.5 Bevis Marks. The resultant publicity did the Jewish cause no harm at all.

At the close of the 18th century there was a small, but growing, fully integrated English-born element within the 18,000 strong London Jewish community. This was accompanied by the emergence of a new spirit of acceptance by general society.

The composer George Friederic Handel arrived in England in 1710 and became rich and famous. Though not himself Jewish, his oratorios portrayed stories from the Hebrew Bible in such works as *Israel in Egypt* and *Joseph and his Brethren*. To the Jews of London these were literal depictions of the glorious deeds of their ancestors. The historian Sir Newman Flower wrote 'A Jew on the stage as a hero rather than a reviled figure was a thing practically unknown in London, and Handel found himself possessed of a new public'. Some have said that the financial success of these works was largely due to the patronage of London Jewry. Handel's compositions were reinforced by

In his play The Jew, *performed in 1794 at the Drury Lane Theatre, Richard Cumberland (1732–1811) became the first playwright in English literature to portray a Jew as a hero. (Courtesy The Jewish Historical Society of England)*

Richard Cumberland's play *The Jew*, first performed in 1794 in Drury Lane. It marked a turning point in English literature in that the main character, Shevan, a Jew, is its hero. He is portrayed as a gold-hearted philanthropist who did good by stealth. Until then, the Jew in drama always had been an unsympathetic character:

> *If your playwriters want a butt, or a buffoon, or a knave to make sport of, out comes the Jew to be baited and buffeted through five long acts for the amusement of all good Christians ...*
>
> *The Jew*, Act 1, Scene 1

Cumberland was followed by others who similarly cast some of their Jewish characters in a more favourable light.

By the time the Napoleonic wars had ended, the position of the Jews had changed for the better. They had performed well in the services. When, in 1803, the arrival of the French fleet was anticipated almost daily, a patriotic wave spread throughout the country. Solomon Hirschell preached in the Great Synagogue urging the congregation to volunteer for the colours and, according to the news sheets, on one day alone 'three hundred of the most respectable individuals of the Jewish persuasion' took the Oath of Allegiance.

Occupations

Jews were becaming increasingly prominent in many callings besides that of financier. Some of the old clothes men and pedlars managed to establish themselves in more respectable walks of life as exporters, manufacturers, tailors, jewellers or shopkeepers. Moses Moses, an old clothes man, leased two shops in Covent Garden, at first dealing in clobbered clothing. Eventually he changed to manufacturing clothing and went into the clothing hire business under the name of Moss Brothers (Moss Bros). Even today the firm supply Ascot-goers with their formal wear.

Henry Mayhew, the social historian, described the East End trading area in his 1851 work *London Labour and the London Poor*:

Jewish hawkers were a familiar sight on London's streets, prepared to buy second hand clothing and other domestic articles. Cartoon c.1840. (By courtesy of the Guildhall Library, Corporation of London)

All these narrow streets, lanes, rows, passages, alleys,

yards, courts, and places, are the sites of the street-trade carried on in this quarter. The whole neighbourhood rings with street cries, many uttered in those strange east-end Jewish tones which do not sound like English ... The savour of the place is moreover peculiar. There is fresh fish, and dried fish, and fish being fried in a style peculiar to the Jews; there is the fustiness of old clothes; there is the odour from the pans on which (still in the Jewish fashion) frizzle and hiss pieces of meat and onions; puddings are boiling and enveloped in steam; cakes with strange names are hot from the oven; tubs of big pickled cucumbers or of onions give a sort of acidity to the atmosphere; lemons and oranges abound; and altogether the scene is not only such as can be seen in London, but only such as can be seen in this part of the metropolis.

Mayhew said the Duke's Place area was 'a large square yard, with the iron gates of a synagogue in one corner, a dead wall forming one entire side of the court, and a gas lamp on a circular pavement in the centre. The place looks as if it were devoted to money-making for it is quiet and dirty. Not a gilt letter is to be seen over a doorway; there is no display of gaudy colour, or sheets of plate glass ... Almost every shop has a scripture name over it, and even the public houses are of the Hebrew faith with a specialised clientele'. There was a 'Jewellers' Arms' used on Sunday mornings where the traders exchanged trinkets and bartered among themselves and the Fishmongers' Arms was 'the resort of the vendors of fried soles', Benjamin's Coffee House was used by old clothes men and Mayhew included an account he was given of their activities:

A view of Long Lane, Smithfield, showing the premises of Morris Solomon, tailor and draper, c.1844. (By courtesy of the Guildhall Library, Corporation of London)

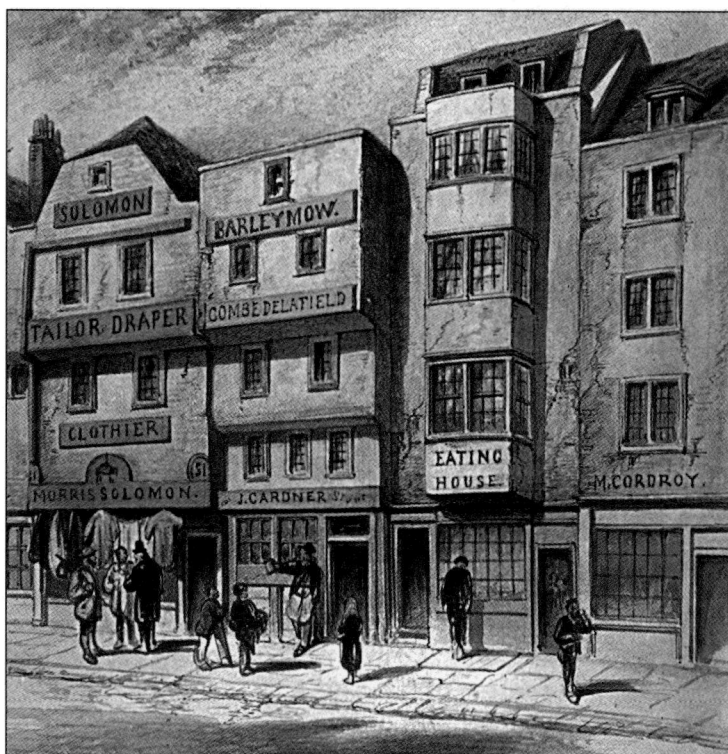

The itinerant Jew Clothes man, he told me, was generally the son of a former old-clothes man, but some were cigar-makers or pencil-makers,

taking to the clothes business when those trades were slack, but that nineteen out of twenty had been born to it. If the parents of the Jew boy are poor, and the boy a sharp lad, he generally commences business at ten years of age, by selling lemons, or some trifle in the streets, and so, as he expressed it, the boy 'gets a round' or street connection, by becoming known to the neighbourhood he visits. If he sees a servant, he will, when selling his lemons, ask if she have any old shoes or old clothes, and offer to be a purchaser. If the clothes should come to more than the Jew boy has in his pocket, he leaves what silver he has as 'an earnest upon them' and then seeks some regular Jew clothes man, who will advance the purchase money. This the old Jew agrees to do upon the understanding that he is to have 'half Rybeck' that is, a moiety of the profit, and then he will accompany the boy to the house, to pass his judgement on the goods, and satisfy himself that the stripling has not made a blind bargain, an error into which he very rarely falls. After this he goes with the lad to Petticoat-lane, and there they share whatever money the clothes may bring over and above what has been paid for them. By such means the Jew boy gets his knowledge of the old-clothes business, and so quick are these lads generally, that in the course of two months they will acquire sufficient experience in connection with the trade to begin dealing on their own account. There are some, he told me, as sharp at 15 as men of 50.

There were Jewish wholesalers in fruit in Duke's Place. The successful manufacturers of cigars, pencils, sealing wax, and importers of sponges and toys, were to be found living in Mansell Street, Great Prescott Street, Great Ailie Street, Leman Street and other parts of Goodman Fields in large private houses. Many were engaged in the wholesale trade in foreign commodities, including shells, tortoises, parrots, birds, curiosities, and ostrich feathers.

One elderly man, who at the time Mayhew saw him was vending spectacles, or bartering them for old clothes, old books, or any second-hand articles, gave him an account of his street life:

He had been in every street-trade, and had on four occasions travelled all over England, selling quills, sealing-wax, pencils, sponges, braces, cheap or superior jewellery, thermometers, and pictures. He had sold barometers in the mountainous parts of Cumberland, been twice to Ireland, and sold a good many quills in Dublin. 'Quills and wax were a great trade with us once: now it's quite different. I've had as much as £60 of my own, and that more than half-a-dozen times, but all of it went in speculations. Yes, some went in gambling'.

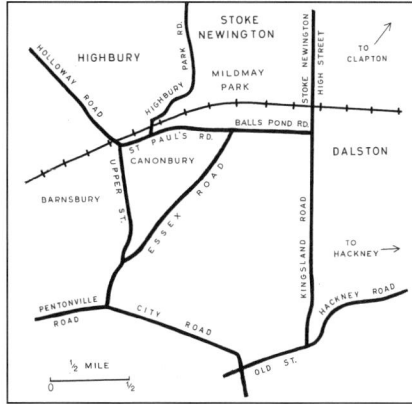

Plan of North London showing areas of migration from the East End in 1880. (Courtesy the Jewish Historical Society of England)

Although Jews were not heavy drinkers, and were rarely drunk, gambling was their great vice.

In the riverside streets from the Tower to Poplar there were Jewish shops catering for seafarers. There were some Jewish-owned boarding houses for sailors in Wapping, but few Jewish street traders worked in the district because they were undersold by the Irish, a more starving body who needed less to live on and so undercut.

There were self-help associations organised by Jewish youths. They

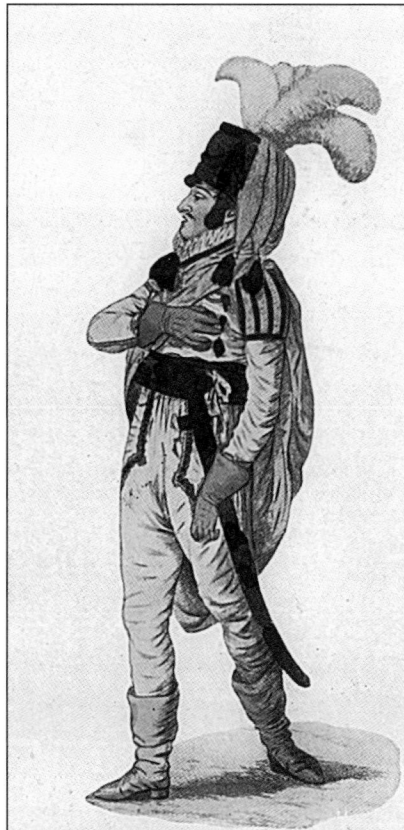

Myer Leoni (d.1796) and John Braham (1774–1856), former members of the choir of the Great Synagogue who both found fame on the stage. Leoni is here shown in costume as Carlos in Sheridan's Duenna *and Braham as Orlando in* As You Like It.

1804. The ketubah (marriage contract) of Isaac Lyon Goldsmid (1778–1859), one of the founders of University College London, and his wife Isabel.

The first Yiddish newspaper published in Britain in 1867.

collected subscriptions of one penny or twopence a week and then gave stock to recommended persons to start up in business. Eighteen shillings was considered enough to set a young man up in trade.

Others had made their marks in many differing fields. David Ricardo (1772–1823), baptised in early manhood, founded a new school of political economy. Benjamin Gompertz (1779–1865) was among the outstanding contemporary mathematicians and actuaries of the day, and Lewis Gomperz was the 'father' of the Royal Society for the Prevention of Cruelty to Animals (RSPCA). Francis Cohen (Palgrave), Isaac D'Israeli (Benjamin Disraeli's father) and others had begun to play a respectable part in English letters. Many went on the stage, including the previously mentioned Myer Leoni, who 'sang like an angel and spoke like a Jew'; to accommodate his religious scruples the performances of Sheridan's comic opera *Duenna*, in which he was appearing at Covent Garden, were suspended on Friday evenings so that he could conduct the services at Bevis Marks. John Braham, his protégé, a prodigious tenor, composer of *The Death of Nelson* and a former choir boy in the Great Synagogue, also did well treading the boards.

At the highest social level were such as the previously mentioned English-born brothers, Benjamin (1755–1808) and Abraham Goldsmid (1756–1810), members of a Dutch family long established in England. They performed financial services for the Government during the war, and were on terms of intimacy with the king's sons, the Dukes of Cumberland, Sussex and Cambridge, whom they entertained in their houses on many occasions and even took to a synagogue service on a Friday evening.

More importantly still, during the later stages of the war Nathan Mayer Rothschild, the founder of the London branch of the banking family, had been brought into an extremely close relationship with the Government as a result of the help he was able to give in providing reliable advanced information of news from abroad. Rothschild's credit system was based on an elaborate intelligence network – his brothers were scattered across Europe; he had agents and couriers all over the South Coast and the facing

ports in Holland; and his servants swarmed over the battlefields of Europe.
The captains of many of the packet boats were also in his pay. He was able to
bring Lord Liverpool, the anxious Prime Minister, the result of the battle at
Waterloo 30 hours before he received the dispatch from Wellington. This was
just one of the many services the family were able to perform for the benefit
of the country.

The Rothschild family, pre-eminent in finance throughout Europe, dominated the leadership of the English community throughout the 19th and into

N.M. Rothschild Esq,
founder of the London
branch of the
Rothschild Bank.

the 20th century, being presidents of this and chairmen of almost everything else. 'Rothschild was a magic name in the Ghetto', wrote Israel Zangwill in his book *Children of the Ghetto,* 'it stands next to the Almighty's as a redresser of grievances and a friend to the poor'. Chaim Bermant observed that 'when the Jews consoled themselves with the expression "the Lord will provide" they usually meant Lord Rothschild'. Both the men and women of the family took leading parts in the establishment and administration of the major Jewish charities – the Jewish Board of Guardians, the United Synagogue and the Jews' Free School among others – and almost invariably headed the lists of charitable donations, both for Jewish and non-Jewish charities. The charity account books held in their archives are a tribute to a remarkably generous family.

The families of the Rothschilds, Cohens, Goldsmids, Montefiores, Samuels and Sassoons, dubbed 'the Cousinhood' by Chaim Bermant because there was so much intermarriage between them, provided most of the community's leaders.

Benjamin Disraeli (1804–1881) is Britain's only Jewish-born Prime Minister. His father, a long-standing member of Bevis Marks, registered Benjamin's birth with the synagogue, but after a quarrel with the Elders in 1814 resigned his membership. In a fit of pique he had his children baptized just as Benjamin was approaching the time of his barmitzvah. Disraeli never denied or disguised his Jewishness – that would have been difficult given his strong Jewish appearance – and continued to be very conscious of his Jewish origins. Until the age of 12 he was brought up as a Jew and received a Jewish education from his grandfather. He did not attend chapel at his school. When his father died, Benjamin sold off his precious library, but not the Jewish books.

Though becoming an adherent of the Church of England – he believed that Christianity was but 'a Judaism for the multitude' – he remained proud of his Jewish heritage and had a strong attachment to his Jewish roots. When, in 1835, he was attacked by a fellow member of Parliament about his Jewish origins he immediately replied, 'Yes. I am a Jew, and when the ancestors of the right honourable gentleman were brutal savages in an unknown island, mine

*Duke's Place
Synagogue in 1809.
(Courtesy Tower
Hamlets Local History
Library and Archives)*

were priests in the Temple of Solomon.' He made an impassioned speech in Parliament in favour of Jewish emancipation in 1847, and maintained his friendship with leading Jewish figures, particularly the Rothschilds. He was invited to their weddings and barmitzvahs and so visited synagogues quite frequently.

In 1875, when he was Prime Minister, he was able to use this contact to the great advantage of the country. A large packet of shares were on offer in the Suez Canal company, the purchase of which would give Britain a much-desired control of the canal. Time was of the essence as other buyers were pressing. Benjamin knew there was only one person he could turn to for ready cash, Baron Lionel de Rothschild. Disraeli's secretary was quickly sent to the Bank and was ushered into the presence of the Baron.

'How much money is needed?' he was asked.

'Four million pounds.'

'When?'

'Tomorrow.'

The Baron was fingering a muscatel grape, popped it into his mouth and spat out the skin.

'What is your security?'

'The British Government.'

'You shall have it.'

Disraeli's cousin, George Basevi (1794–1845), an architect, also had a distinguished career, and was perhaps best known for designing the Fitzwilliam Museum in Cambridge and Cadogan Square in Belgravia.

Municipal and Parliamentary Emancipation

Though there had certainly been progress socially and economically, the Jews still suffered from many civil disabilities. Ever since 1534, when Henry VIII declared himself to be head of the Church in place of the Pope, it was maintained that the Church of England espoused the only true form of religion. The very existence of the State, it was asserted, was dependent on this principle, and therefore no state duties could be entrusted to anyone who was not a member. The Test and Corporation Act of 1673 prescribed that all government officials, civil and military, had to take the oath according to the forms of the established church. As a result, Jews and nonconformists (including Roman Catholics) were barred from every avenue of public service, municipal and parliamentary. Jews could not be called to the Bar, or take degrees at Oxford or Cambridge, and were thus virtually excluded from the professions. They could not hold high rank in the Army. Their claims for emancipation were persistently and vigorously opposed. It was said that their admission would 'un-Christianise' the State.

The establishment of University College in Gower Street in 1826 (it was originally named London University), was a notable landmark for Anglo-Jewry. It had strong financial support from members of the community, particularly from Sir Isaac Lyon Goldsmid, and allowed entry to adherents of every religion or none. Hyman Hurwitz, a Talmudic scholar, was appointed the first Professor of Hebrew in 1825. Today there is a strong Department of Jewish Studies at the college.

It was not until 1828 that the Test Acts were repealed and a year later that the disabilities of Roman Catholics were swept away by the Catholic Emancipation Act. Unfortunately for the

University College, London. Jews were barred from obtaining degrees at Oxford and Cambridge. London University, founded in 1826, was non-denominational and enabled Jews and other nonconformists to obtain degrees, and opened their way to the professions.

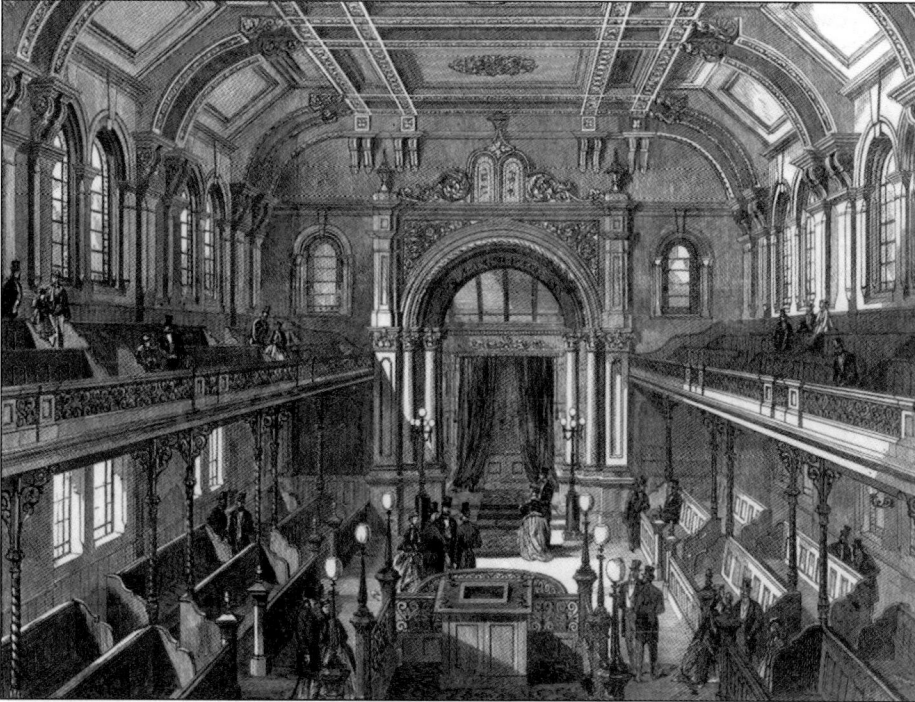

Borough Synagogue, Walworth Road, May 1867. The Borough School adjoined it.

Reconsecration service at the Western Synagogue at St Alban's Place in April 1851. (Courtesy David Jacobs)

Great St Helen's in 1855, recently repaired and redecorated following a fire that partially destroyed it. 'The finest synagogue in Europe' according to the Illustrated Times.

Jews, though they had taken an active part in the agitation against the Test Acts, they gained nothing by their repeal; on the contrary the House of Lords had insisted that the words 'on the true faith of a Christian' should be part of the revised Oath of Allegiance, thereby continuing the exclusion of Jews from sitting in Parliament.

Nonetheless, given the improved general situation, the time seemed right to attempt to remedy the position. The community, however, was divided. Most preferred to let sleeping dogs lie, concerned about the consequences that protests and public agitation might produce and afraid of

Another view of the Central Synagogue in Great Portland Street, May 1870.

arousing anti-Semitism. There was a conflict of aspirations among the leaders. Some who were engaged in the retail trade would have been completely satisfied if they were allowed to carry on their business within the Square Mile. The wealthier Jews had still less to complain of, and were not eager for a fight because their social emancipation was virtually completed, and they were in no hurry for political emancipation. Sir Moses Montefiore (1784–1859) and others were prepared to compromise and accept less than full emancipation – at least as an interim measure – though Sir Moses made it clear that he was firmly determined not to give up the smallest part of his Judaism to obtain civil rights. Yet others were adamant that the immediate aim should be full emancipation. The consequence of this conflict of views within their ranks was that Jews had to wait much longer than they had expected, and emancipation was achieved in piecemeal fashion.

In the early 1820s Isaac Lyon Goldsmid, a wealthy merchant banker, who had helped to finance the London docks, the railways and University College, stood almost alone in the emancipation struggle, but his efforts to raise the Jewish question through the press and pamphlets gained a cordial reception. By 1830 he had formed an association to organise the agitation. Its honorary secretary was Barnard Van Oven, a son of Joshua Van Oven. They succeeded in securing the co-operation of men who were influential in public and political life, and despite meeting deep and bitter opposition the crusade found

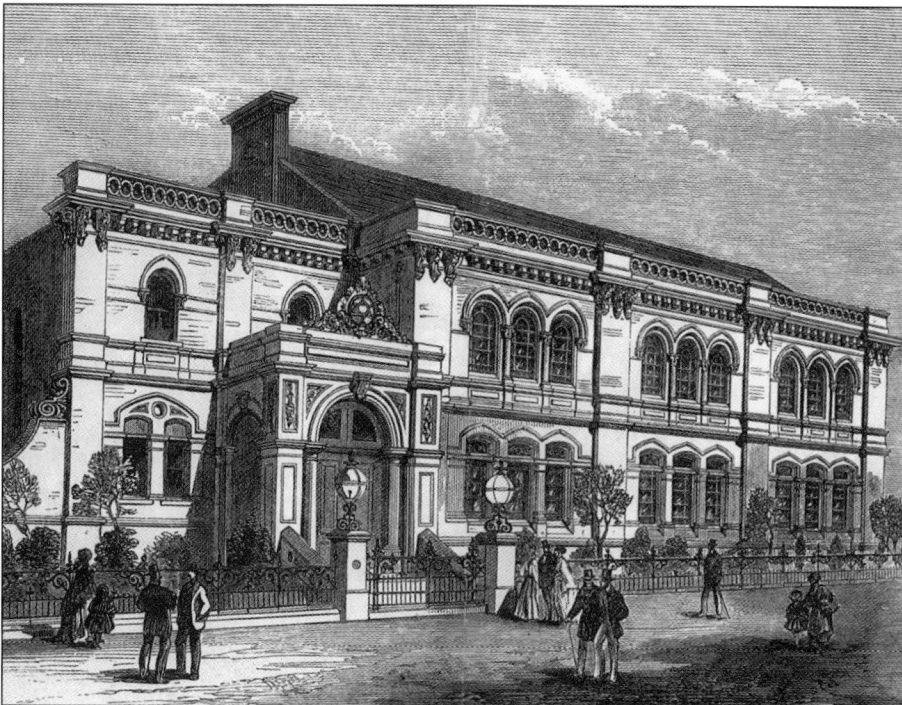

The new building of the Barnsbury Synagogue in October 1868. The interior decorative plastering of fig, vine, palm and corn was modelled on samples in Kew Botanical Gardens.

*Sir David Salomons
(1797–1873), the first
Jewish Lord Mayor,
1855.*

*Nathan Marcus Adler
(1803–91) of Hanover.
Chief Rabbi from
1845–91, he was
succeeded by his son
Hermann Adler.*

many Gentile supporters The service of Jews in the armed forces during the war, and the synagogue prayers including one for the well-being of the Royal Family, provided confirmation of their patriotism.

The campaign initially concentrated on the restrictions imposed in the City of London. In 1830, the Common Council enacted that henceforth any person who applied to become a freeman of the City of London could make the necessary oath in a form agreeable to his religious convictions. This meant not only that Jews could now become freemen, but also that they could carry on trade in the city and be members of livery companies. David Salomons (1793–1873), a well-known City figure and one of the founders of the Westminster Bank, whose family had for three generations played their part in the affairs of the Anglo-Jewish community, had ambitions in public life, and he successfully applied for membership of the Coopers' Company and proceeded rapidly from one civic dignity to another.

In 1835, despite some opposition on religious grounds, he was elected Sheriff, but the statutory declaration 'on the true faith of a Christian' made it impossible for him to take up the position. To solve the difficulty Parliament promptly passed the Sheriff's Declaration Act, making special provision for persons elected to this office. In 1837 Moses Montefiore became Sheriff of London and was knighted by Queen Victoria on the occasion of her state visit to the city after her coronation, becoming the first Jew since Sir Solomon Medina to receive that distinction.

In 1845 all the City offices were thrown open to Jews, and in 1855 Salomons became Lord Mayor. There have been just seven Jewish Lord Mayors since then: Benjamin Phillips in 1865, Harry Isaacs in

1889, George Faudel-Phillips in 1896, Marcus Samuel (later Lord Bearstead) in 1902, Samuel Joseph (father of Sir Keith Joseph) in 1942, Bernard Waley-Cohen in 1960, and Peter Levene in 1998. When Marcus Samuel took up office he arranged for the Lord Mayor's procession to start an hour earlier than usual so that it could start in and pass through part of the immigrant area. A special stand was erected outside St Botolph's Church in Aldgate for the Lady

Sir George Faudel-Phillips, Lord Mayor of London in 1896, was the first son to follow his father to the honour.

Mayoress and her party. The band of the Jews' Orphan Society played there. For many of the refugee immigrants it was the first time they could feel they really belonged to the country that had taken them in, for in every street was the Lord Mayor of London showing himself to them, accompanied by the Household Cavalry, the Brigade of Guards, the State Trumpeters, the whole history of England displayed in the glitter and pomp of the occasion, and all there to honour one man, a Jew like themselves.

Members of Parliament were required to take the Oath of Allegiance 'on the true faith of a Christian'. In 1858 Baron Lionel de Rothschild became the first Jewish Member admitted to Parliament after these words were no longer required.

The marriage at the Central Synagogue in January 1881 of Leopold de Rothschild and Marie Perugia, at which the Prince of Wales was a guest.

Walter Rothschild (1868–1937), a naturalist and collector. He trained the zebras who were stabled, groomed, fed and shod in the same way as horses, and drove them in Hyde Park.

Other aims were also achieved. In 1833, Francis Goldsmid became the first Jew to be called to the Bar and was appointed a Queen's Counsel in 1858. In 1841, Sir Isaac Lyon Goldsmid became a baronet, the first Jew to be awarded a hereditary title. Sir George Jessel was the first Jewish judge, and, in 1885, Lord Rothschild the first Jewish peer.

On the parliamentary front, between 1830 and 1858 there were no fewer than 14 attempts to remove Jewish disabilities. The first Bill was rejected by the House of Commons, while the next 12 passed the Commons but were rejected by the House of Lords. Both Baron Lionel de Rothschild (his title was Austrian) and David Salomons stood for and were elected to Parliament, but they were ordered to withdraw from the House after refusing to take the oath in the prescribed form. On one occasion, in 1851, Salomons ignored the instruction to withdraw, took part in a debate, and recorded his vote three times before the sergeant-at-arms arrived to remove him. He was subsequently fined. In 1858 the 14th Bill proved acceptable – and the battle was won. Baron de Rothschild was elected and took his seat.

Where they lived

In 1800, the overwhelming majority of London's
Jews, rich and poor, were still living in the East
End of London, in and around the City. Some
prosperous families were further east in Bow and
some who had shops or traded as ship's chan-
dlers among the Irish in Shadwell and Limehouse
lived there. But it was in Wentworth Street and
Middlesex Street, Butler Street, Thrawl Street,
Fashion Street and Flower and Dean Street and the surrounding streets within
the Spitalfields area, formerly occupied by the Huguenot weavers, that the
majority lived.

Wedding of the Earl of Rosebery and Hannah Rothschild at Mount Street Registry Office in 1878. The bride was given away by the Prime Minister,, the Earl of Beaconsfield

   The movement away from the East End was a gradual process, led by the
wealthy. In the 1830s the well-to-do started to move to Finsbury Square and
Finsbury Circus, and the streets between them. This comparatively small area
held five percent of the Jewish upper and middle-class families. It was, however, too near the City synagogues to produce a separate synagogue or communal life of its own.

   The Rothschilds had their own urban 'ghetto' in Piccadilly. In 1825 Nathan
Mayer Rothschild bought No.107; Ferdinand was to be found at No.143;
Alice at No.142; Hannah, who married the Prime Minister Lord Rosebery,
took over No.107; Lionel built No.148 next to Apsley House in the 1860s,
and Leopold was at No.5 Hamilton Place. In 1825, Moses Montefiore moved
to Green Street and shortly afterwards to No.99 Park Lane. Isaac Lyon
Goldsmid went to Regents Park. Disraeli's town house from 1839–73 was
No.93 Park Lane. When the *Jewish Chronicle,* the oldest continuously printed

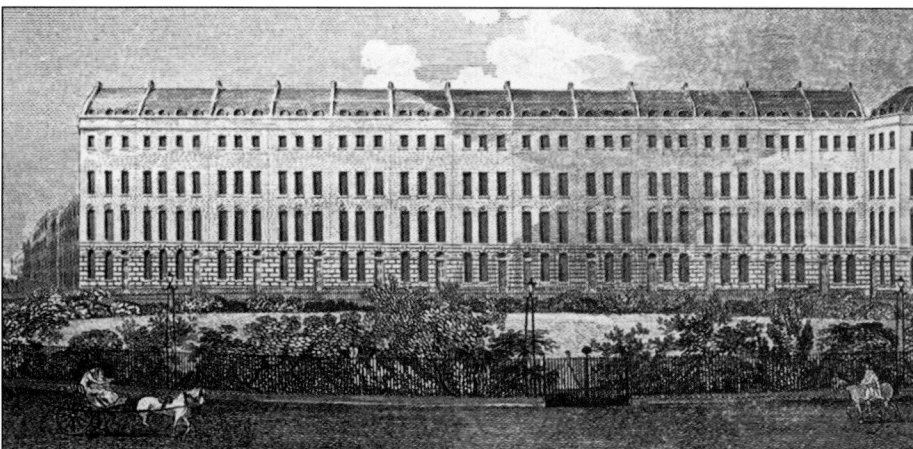

Finsbury Square became a fashionable area for the Jewish well-to-do from the 1830s. (Courtesy Guildhall Library, Corporation of London)

Baron Rothschild's new mansion adjoining Apsley House in 1862.

Sir Henry Aaron Isaacs (1830–1909). Lord Mayor of London in 1889, a fruit and steamship broker in Eastcheap and Hull. Two of his daughters were born deaf and dumb and he became a recognised authority on the oral system of teaching deaf mutes.

Jewish newspaper in the world, was first published in 1841, there were sufficient prospective subscribers in the West End for it to appoint two of its five distributors there, one in the Strand and one in Soho. By the 1840s the large Mocatta family had settled in the West End in and around Russell Square.

The middle class went to Islington in the 1840s, and the villas laid out in Highbury after 1850 attracted many, their spacious grounds earning it the title of 'the Mayfair of Islington'. The Maida Vale area attracted a very considerable middle-class Jewish settlement; in the 1880s 20 per cent of Maida Vale's 10,000 residents were Jewish.

For a time Hackney was the resort of the upper middle class, but by 1842 very few remained there. The expanding railway system made it financially possible for the poorer section of London society to work in London but to live in this hitherto middle-class preserve. By the mid-1890s it was being described in the *Jewish Chronicle* as 'a district thickly populated by the better class of Jewish working men'.

Moves further westward towards Bayswater started in the 1860s. The Bayswater Synagogue opened in 1863. There was a later development of a more proletarian congregation in Notting Hill and Shepherds Bush.

The development of the northern part of St John's Wood, and in Hampstead

between Finchley Road and Fitzjohn's Avenue, became the favourite area of the scholarly and the intellectuals. At the end of the 19th century Charles Booth wrote of Hampstead: 'the old families leave, the Jews come, the artistic and Bohemian element prevails'. Abbey Road Synagogue opened in 1882 and the Hampstead Synagogue in Dennington Park Road in 1892. A synagogue was established in Chevening Road, Brondesbury, in 1900.

The Jews living south of the Thames were, and remain to this day, a very important, but comparatively small, minority.

Top left: Sir Moses Montefiore on his 99th birthday in 1883.

Top right: 9 November 1837: Her Majesty Queen Victoria knighting Sir Moses Montefiore.

Israel Zangwill (1864–1926). Playwright, Zionist and author. In 1892 he wrote Children of the Ghetto, *a book that vividly described Jewish East End life.*

Synagogues and the Reform Movement

The westward drift of the Jewish population caused considerable concern to the East End synagogues: Bevis Marks, the Great, the Hambro and the New. They feared that if the wealthy formed their own synagogues in the West End the financial burden on those who remained in the East End could become overwhelming. They were worried that the East End community might not be able to maintain its collective responsibilities for the welfare of the poor, the burial of the dead, or even the upkeep of its own buildings. To avoid fragmentation they dug their heads in the sand and embarked upon a Canute-like policy of trying to restrain the movement. They forbad their members to hold or even attend services anywhere within six miles of the existing synagogues (10 miles in the case of the Great).

Appeals made by those living in the West End to the elders and clergy of Bevis Marks and the Great to open synagogues in the West End were ignored. The elders' response was to do nothing and hope that somehow the clamour would die down. It was an impossible position to maintain because the tide of fashion and wealth was flowing strongly westwards.

The home of Abraham Goldsmid in Morden, Surrey, 1806. (Courtesy Guildhall Library, Corporation of London)

The new West Enders thought it wrong that they should either have to forgo the pleasures of communal worship or walk several miles to the synagogue. They had other complaints too: in their view the services were too long, held at inconvenient hours, and observed in an unimpressive manner. Many disliked the inattentiveness of worshippers, the sale of special prayers (*misheberach*), and congregational behaviour that they considered 'more suited to the coffee house or exchange'. Sir Moses Montefiore and a few others were content to make the four and a half mile journey on foot, but they were a very small

Whitechapel High Street, 1837.

minority. Some stayed away from the existing synagogues, and others withdrew completely from both the community and religion.

After a long period of gestation the reform movement in England was
established on 15 April 1840. The declaration that heralded its arrival was
signed by 24 gentlemen, 19 Sephardim and five Ashkenazim, at a meeting
in the Bedford Hotel in Russell Square. Nearly all the founders were
members of old established elite Jewish families, the significant omission
being the Rothschilds.

The reformers proposed the writing of a new prayer book, a revised order
of service, and the inclusion of a sermon in English, all suggestions that were
considered heretical and only served to increase the distrust and consternation
of the East End elders. In September 1841, Chief Rabbi Solomon Hirschell –

The Jews' Hospital
opened in the Mile End
Road in 1806 and
moved to Norwood in
1863.

with the backing and indeed at the instigation of Bevis Marks – issued a *herem* (excommunication) against the new community, which was publicly read out by the respective secretaries in the Great and other Jewish places of worship in London (except at the Western which, in keeping with its independence, refused to do so).

The resolve of the reformers remained undiminished. A minister, Revd Professor David Woolf Marks, a former Jews' Free School pupil, was appointed, and a synagogue was consecrated on 27 January 1842 in Burton Street, Bloomsbury (situated between Upper Woburn Place and Cartwright Gardens). The new congregation called itself the the West London Synagogue of British Jews.

For months the issue of the reform schism dominated the headlines of the *Jewish Chronicle*. The paper backed the communal establishment, but was at the same time careful not to offend the sensibilities of the reform congregation.

Founded in 1841 it is the oldest Jewish newspaper in existence. Its early editions devoted considerable space to the development of the Reform movement.

THE JEWISH CHRONICLE

"A word in its season how good it is." Proverbs, chap. 15, ver. 23,

No. 1.]   NOVEMBER 12th, 5602.—1841.   [PRICE 2d.

TO OUR READERS.
We have always anticipated the appearance of a truly Jewish paper, with the most lively satisfaction; for we knew, that the existence among us, of an organ of mutual communication, was a desideratum of such magnitude, that the person

to our publication, the less matter of fact, but not less honorable productions of their well stored minds; indeed, we have already received a tale, which we purpose commencing at the earliest opportunity.

4thly.   Our Text Books will not, we dare venture to assert, form the least

Initially the *herem* created problems with regard to marriages and burials. Under the Marriage Registration Act of 1836 synagogues were allowed to perform marriages after giving notice to the registrar and obtaining the appropriate certificate. The stumbling block for the reformers was that they first needed confirmation from the Board of Deputies that they were a recognised place of worship. Sir Moses Montefiore, who was President of the Board and closely connected with Bevis Marks, opposed the new synagogue and refused to grant it recognition. As a result, members had to have civil marriages conducted by a registrar followed by a ceremony under the *chuppa* (canopy) in the synagogue.

The *herem* also barred the congregation from the existing burial grounds. In 1843, the West London opened its own grounds in Balls Pond Road,

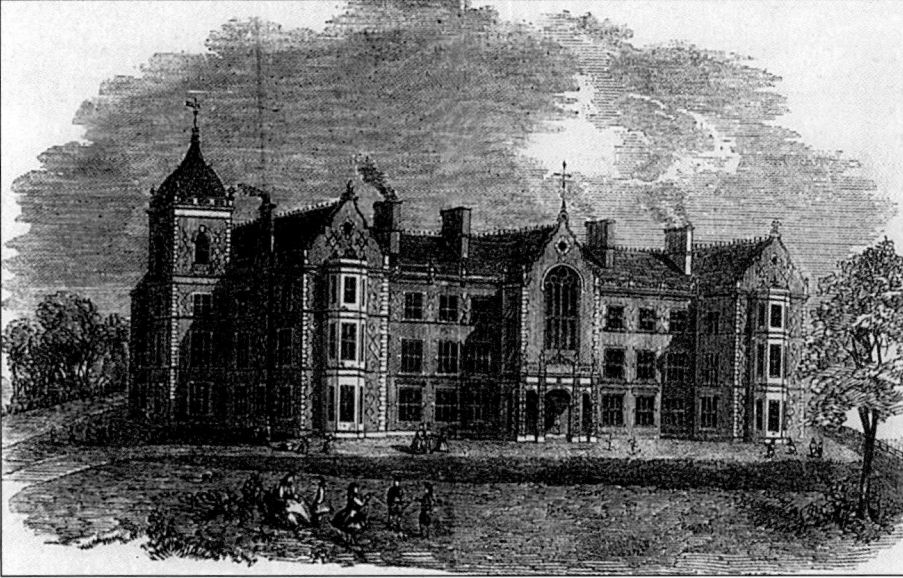

Dalston. Long since closed for interments, it contains the graves of many of the leading lights of the early days of the movement.

The congregation soon outgrew the Burton Street building and in June 1849 moved into a larger synagogue at 50 Margaret Street near Oxford Circus. Shortly before the new building's consecration the *herem* was removed. The problem of marriages was overcome in 1856 when the West London obtained a Marriage Act of its own, making it independent of the Board of Deputies.

The congregation continued to grow, and in 1870 a new larger synagogue was opened in Upper Berkeley Street. Its fees were high for the time, £7 annually for men and £3 for women, and its membership was derived not from the West End working-class element who lived in Soho, but from residents of Bloomsbury, Marylebone and Mayfair. The largest single occupation of the bridegrooms married in the synagogue was 'merchant', followed by stockbrokers, jobbers and professional men. Professor Marks served the congregation for 54 years and held the Chair of Hebrew at University College. In 1900, the 32 members of its Council included five Henriques, three Mocattas, three Montefiores and two Waleys.

The magnificent interior of the present building reflects its origins. The strong Moorish influence in the great arches of the interior and cupola above the Ark are eloquent reminders of the Sephardi background of the founding fathers of the synagogue. One of the most beautiful of the Victorian synagogues, it continues to flourish with a membership of more than 1,800 families, only a small percentage of whom live in the West End.

Eventually, the East End synagogues bowed to the inevitable. Bevis Marks

The Watch Fair in Houndsditch in 1865.

Sir Benjamin Phillips (1811–1889), the second Jewish Lord Mayor. He rose from humble beginnings to become a member of a successful City firm of importers and manufacturers of embroidery and fancy wool.

opened a branch at No.4 Wigmore Street in 1853 and then moved to Upper Bryanston Street by Marble Arch in 1861. It finally moved to Lauderdale Road, Maida Vale, in 1896, where it continues to flourish.

The Great Synagogue was slower to react. When at last there were no excuses for further procrastination, it took the lease of a warehouse in Portland Street and adapted it for synagogue use. On 29 March 1855, six and a half years after the proposal had first been approved, the new place of worship, the Central Synagogue, was inaugurated. The inordinate delay had, of course, given the West London Reform synagogue valuable time in which to consolidate itself in the community in general, and the West End in particular.

Once again, this was a synagogue for the wealthy. Its Building Committee included Sir Anthony de Rothschild, Lionel Cohen, Jacob Waley, Ephraim Alex, Samuel Montagu, Alderman (later Lord Mayor) Benjamin Phillips and Henry de Worms, all luminaries of Anglo-Jewry. In 1870, of the eight Jewish Members of Parliament, five were members of the Central Synagogue. The Central continued to be one of the wealthiest congregations in London, but as the century progressed it was surpassed by the New West End, Bayswater and Hampstead synagogues.

The original building was superseded in 1870 by another in Great Portland Street. When Sir Anthony de Rothschild married Mademoiselle Marie Perugia there in January 1881, the Prince of Wales and Lord Rosebery were among the guests and sat with Alfred and Nathaniel Rothschild in the warden's box. It became one of the great cathedral synagogues of Anglo-Jewry and remained so until 10 May 1941, when it was destroyed by German bombing. With generous support from the Isaac Wolfson family and others, the new Central was completed in 1958. Until the end of the 1960s it retained much of its influence, but since then, with more than 80 percent of its congregation living outside the area, it has declined and its future is uncertain.

The United Synagogue

During the first half of the 19th century, the burden of caring for the poor still fell most heavily on the three Ashkenazi synagogues, the Great, the Hambro and the New. In 1834, mainly on the initiative of Nathan Mayer Rothschild, a treaty was entered into between them to establish a permanent working relationship and to apportion the tasks and financial contribution that each should make to secure the welfare of the poor. With the opening of the Bayswater and Central Synagogues, it became clear that there could be advantages to having a central body with regulations covering all five synagogues. A private Act of Parliament establishing the United Synagogue was passed in 1870. Its provisions allow for the admission of other existing synagogues and the erection of new synagogues under the United Synagogue's auspices. The form of worship and all religious observances are under the supervision and control of the Chief Rabbi, and these have to be in accordance with the Ashkenazi ritual. No marriage can be solemnized and no person can conduct a religious service within the United Synagogue without his consent. The United Synagogue remains the embodiment of mainstream Judaism in Britain. Today, there are 43 member synagogues and 21 affiliated synagogues, providing facilities for 30,000 families.

Welfare of the Poor

During the 19th century primary responsibility for social welfare lay with voluntary agencies, particularly in health, education and housing. It was the philanthropists who funded new hospitals, schools, universities and universi-

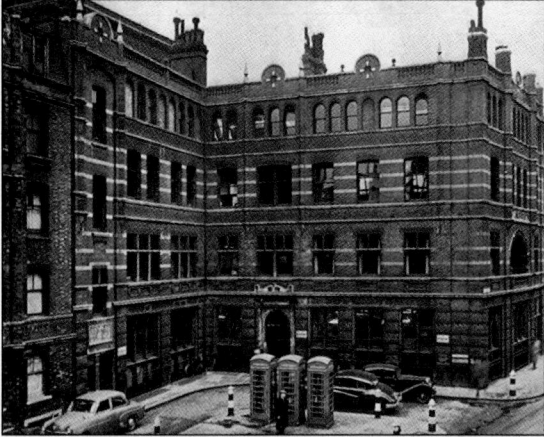

The Jewish Board of Guardians' offices were in Middlesex Street from 1896 to 1957.

ty colleges; and it was they who financed medical and scientific research and established libraries, museums, art galleries, public parks and urban housing experiments. Facilities provided by the state were largely supplementary to their efforts. At that time Parliament followed but rarely initiated social reform.

The Victorians were great organisers of charity, but it is fair to say that British Victorian Jewry excelled at it. They equalled or surpassed their neighbours in the number, variety and quality of their charitable bodies, an activity that was rooted in the Jewish religious concept of charity as a positive obligation.

With just a few notable exceptions it was the Jewish upper and middle classes who provided the Jewish welfare bodies with financial support, directly by subscription, gifts and legacies, or indirectly by subventions from synagogues.

For much of the 19th century the Jewish rich and poor lived near each other, or prayed in the same synagogue, so the former could not be blind to the wants of the latter. As the century progressed, and with it the exodus away from the East End, ties were loosened. Lionel Louis Cohen wrote in 1860 that the situation of the East End poor had deteriorated as a result of this development:

> *Formerly when rich and poor lived in close proximity, every man was himself almost a Board of Guardians; he knew and came continually into contact with the poor and if he inclined to overlook their wants, he could not do so; they were close to his own door, and could and did exhort by clamour and absolute and continued solicitation the relief of that distress which to most of us is now known only by report.*

There was a society for providing for the wants of the Jewish poor at every stage from the cradle to the grave, and by Victorian standards they were quite generous. There were Jewish loan societies, soup kitchens, clothing associations, and societies for the distribution of bread and fuel tickets. The Jewish Blind Society had been established as early as 1819, and the *Jewish Chronicle* claimed in 1842 that 'now, happily, there does not remain in the metropolis a single blind Jew requiring aid without a stipend for life'. The Jews' Deaf and Dumb Home opened in 1865; a Home and Hospital for Jewish Incurables at Nightingale Lane, Tottenham, in 1889; and a convalescent home for tuberculosis sufferers at Daneswood in 1905.

The Orange Market in Duke's Place in 1850.

The Hand in Hand (1840) and the Widows' Home (1843) were grass roots charities founded by working men and women for the relief of distress of their own class. Their primary function was to save the aged poor from starvation and exposure on the streets or having to endure the terrible conditions of the workhouse, and to allow them to practise and die in their faith. Chief Rabbi Nathan Adler said they gave help to those who had reached that age at which, as the Jewish sages had described it, 'the hills become mountains, the neighbour's house a great distance, and we seek things we have not lost'.

Ephraim Alex (1800–1882), founder and first President of the Jewish Board of Guardians from 1859–1869.

Another working-class movement started by Solomon Green (1830–99) led to the establishment in 1871 of a Jewish workhouse at No.123 Wentworth Street that later moved to Stepney Green. All three organisations eventually amalgamated and moved to spacious accommodation in Nightingale Lane, Wandsworth, the gift of Lord Wandsworth. Nightingale House, as it is known today, is the largest home of its type in Europe, catering for 300 residents in conditions that incorporate the most advanced ideas in care for the older person. The present Chief Rabbi, Professor Jonathan Sacks, wrote 'Societies are judged by how they treat their most valuable members: the very young and the very old. By those standards Nightingale House is a shining example. And what a difference it makes to its residents! It may or may not add years to their lives, but one thing is certain: it adds life to their years.'

The Jewish Board of Guardians

In 1859, growing discontent with the fragmented state of Jewish charity – and the suffering caused by the severe winter of 1848–9 – prompted the leaders of the three Ashkenazi City Synagogues to establish a centralised relief agency, the Jewish Board of Guardians.

Operating from Middlesex Street under the guidance of its moving spirit, the banker and stockbroker Lionel Louis Cohen (1832–87), its first objective was to remove relief from the scope of the individual syna-

December 1879: soup kitchen for the Jewish poor. Originally opened in 1854 in Leman Street, it later moved to Black Lion Yard, then Fashion Street and in 1903 to Brune Street.

gogue congregations because they were too restricted as units of organisation, and to transfer it to the local Jewish community as a whole. The larger unit also made possible the employment of paid staff, who could help the voluntary workers carry out a thorough investigation of the circumstances and needs of each applicant.

It slowly expanded the scope of its work, rationalising, consolidating, abolishing indiscriminate almsgiving, and helping the poor to help themselves. However, lest it be thought they were encouraging migrants to come to London, a ruling was made that the Board would not assist any applicant who had not been resident in the country for at least six months, unless the application was for money to enable an immediate return to the country of origin.

The Board engaged in effective sanitary work by appointing its own inspectors; was active in preventing the spread of tuberculosis; arranged apprenticeships; made small loans to help men to start in business; hired sewing machines to tailors and dressmakers and enabled workers in other trades – glaziers, carpenters, cabinetmakers, shoemakers, printers and bookbinders – to purchase tools and equipment on a similar basis. It stimulated local authori-

Moses Square, 1865, 'where the rags and tatters, and second-hand hats and bonnets, and shoes and stockings, were bartered and haggled'.

Interior of the Great Synagogue, c.1850, during the autumn festival of Succoth. (Courtesy Guildhall Library, Corporation of London)

ties to take statutory action against landlords who did not fulfil their obligations to carry out repairs, and badgered defaulting landlords directly. It carries on its work today under the name Jewish Care.

As will be discussed, the community had also made special arrangements to ensure adequate medical and hospital care for its sick poor.

Between 1869 and 1882 the Board dealt on average with over 2,000 cases a year, represent-

An interior view, c.1830, of the Royal Exchange. The Jews on the Exchange congregated in the south-east corner, under the colonnade. It was known as 'Jews' Walk'. (Courtesy Guildhall Library, Corporation of London)

ing families totalling 7,000 to 8,000 persons, or about 20 to 25 percent of the London Jewish population.

There were many spheres in which Jewish charitable institutions were in the vanguard of progress – in care for the blind and the deaf, home helps for pregnant and nursing mothers, health visiting, care for schoolchildren, and in the fight against tuberculosis and poor sanitation. The Jews' Deaf and Dumb Home, opened in Whitechapel in 1865, was one of the pioneers in this country of the oral and lip reading system.

By 1880, leading the community were some 200 households whose wealth derived from finance-related activity – merchant banking, commodity and stock brokerage, foreign loans and currency and bullion transactions. Almost half the remainder came within the category of middle class (those with family incomes of £1,000 or more). Below them were the working class, and those among them who fell on difficult times were cushioned against the problems of everyday life by the charitable organizations described above.

The community considered itself relatively compact and well-organised, and felt that full integration was in sight. This proved to be a false sense of security. The edifice that had been erected was to be put in danger. The community was about to have its whole world turned upside down.

Chapter 6

1881–1914:
The Avalanche

WHAT had been a steady stream of immigration became a raging flood following the assassination of Tsar Alexander II on 1 March 1881. The English Jewish community's peaceful calm was shattered; they were swamped by the new arrivals who outnumbered them by three to one. In consequence the existing small community underwent a profound change in both its structure and its character. It brought about a situation of an altogether different dimension, causing severe problems for both the host and the Jewish community.

The arrival of immigrants at St Katherine's Dock. Customs officers are examining their meagre luggage.

Between 1880 and 1914 there was an exodus of almost three million Jews from Eastern Europe, including two million from Russia and Poland, 450,000 from Austro-Hungary, and 150,000 from Romania. Just over two million went to America, while 150,000 settled in Britain. Others went to South Africa and South America.

To appreciate who the new arrivals were, and why they came, it is necessary to understand their Eastern European background and experience. Life was never easy for Jews in Russia; its government was arbitrary, authoritarian and persecutory. One of the greatest hardships Jews faced there was that conditions alternated violently back and forth between periods of relative tolerance and calm and periods of reaction and repression, depending upon who was occupying the throne. This led to a continuous state of anxiety and insecurity, fed and sustained by popular violence, propaganda, and discrimination.

The reign of the tyrannical and merciless Tsar Nicholas I between 1825 and 1855 was especially savage. Under his jurisdiction more than 600 anti-Jewish edicts were written into law. These ranged from the mildly annoying – censorship of Jewish texts and newspapers and rules that restricted the curricula of Jewish schools, to the monstrous – expulsion from homes and villages, confiscation of property, and a decree binding boys between the ages of 12 and 25 to service in the Russian Army for 25 years. The object of this Iron Tsar was to remove all traces of

1896: many immigrant arrivals in London travelled on to America.

Many immigrants brought their bedding and even crockery with them, but very little money.

Poster advertising a protest meeting against the treatment of the Jews in Russia in 1890. Note the many non-Jewish supporters.

The ecclesiastical authorities exercised strict supervision over the sale of kosher meat and poultry.

Judaism from his Tsardom; to purify and Christianise it. There were echoes in this of the state of Anglo-Jewry in mediaeval times.

The accession of Alexander II in 1855 came as a relief. He was advised by his ministers that restrictions on Jews were not only unjust, but harmful to Russia's economic interests, and concessions were made. He permitted some Jewish youths to enter Russian universities. A few Jewish businessmen whom he found useful were allowed to travel in parts of Russia from which they had previously been prohibited. There was a modest relaxation of the heavy taxes imposed on Jews, and the period of compulsory conscription was reduced to five years. But the reign of his successor, Alexander III, was marked by relentless hostility. His 'May Laws' of 1882 prohibited Jews from owning or renting land outside towns and cities, discouraged them from living in villages and prohibited them from engaging in work on Sundays and Christian holidays. In that year 500,000 Jews in rural areas were forced to leave their homes and live in towns or townlets (*shtetls*) in the Pale of Settlement, the 15 western and southern provinces of Russia and the Kingdom of Poland stretching from Yalta in the south to Kovno in the north, from Warsaw in the west to Chernigov in the east. Jews were confined there by law, resulting in intolerable overcrowding and few economic opportunities. By the end of the century, 40 percent of Jews in that area were living wholly or partly on charity, and it was said of Vilna that 80 percent of the Jewish population did not know in the evening how and where they would obtain food the next morning.

The Jews were blamed for Alexander's death, though only one of the five conspirators was Jewish, a young seamstress named Jessie Helfmann, later hanged. There was an attack on Jews at Elisavetgrad, and a wave of terror spread through the provinces of Kiev, Chernigov, Poltava, Kherson and Ekaterinoslav. Pogroms began in the Ukraine and continued sporadically until 1884, mainly confined to Southern Russia. Four years later, Jews were forbidden to move from one village to another without a special permit. In 1891 they were expelled from Moscow and Kiev, and in 1899 an economic crisis in Bessarabia and Kherson led to famine and riots. There were further pogroms in Kishinev in 1903, followed by one of the worst, in Odessa, in 1905.

For Jews, the Pale of Settlement had become a land of severe social and economic deprivation and religious persecution, and they were forced to consider emigration. They decided to leave in order to escape the pogroms (or fear of them), the grinding poverty, a corrupt bureaucracy, and the restrictions on their lives. They left because they were hungry, because they were persecuted, and because life in Russia had become intolerable. An immigrant tailor explained his motives, which were, he believed, typical of many others:

> I did not leave my native country because I was expelled … but because nearly every day brought me news of new laws against the people of my race; and I was asking myself, Where is this going to stop? Whose turn will be next? And I decided to leave the country where I could get neither justice nor mercy.

They came weekly by steamer from Libau, Hamburg, Rotterdam and Bremen. Most landed in London having encountered perils at every stage of the journey, from home to the port, on the sea voyage, and at the port of disembarkation. A passport was officially required to leave Russia but it was expensive and surrounded by bureaucracy. Many left without one, often accompanied by local guides who charged heavily and sometimes deserted them. Many were fleeced by keepers of immigrant hostels, railway employees, ships' officers and crews, and by the ticket agents. Stolen baggage, exorbitant lodging rates, misrepresentation of ships' facilities and changes of sailing schedules occurred daily. Some were sold tickets for the wrong destination, for

Advertisement by the Four Per Cent Dwelling Company for their flats in Stoke Newington.

London for example instead of New York.

Conditions on board during the three days passage from Hamburg to Tilbury were poor. Many who strictly observed the rules of *kashrut* survived on herrings and potatoes. They all arrived dishevelled, often dirty and with their clothes in tatters. Many had not changed their clothing since they left home, perhaps weeks before, on the long journey.

At the port of disembarkation they could be picked up by other sharks, with the addition, in the early days, of white slave traffickers looking for young girls travelling alone.

MORE ROOM TO LIVE!

CHEAP RENTS.

SPACIOUS, COMMODIOUS

FLATS

OF

2 ROOMS | **4 ROOMS**
3 ROOMS | **5 ROOMS**

In each case with Scullery, Separate w.c., Balcony, &c.

TO BE LET

ON THE

COMPANY'S NEW ESTATE, STOKE NEWINGTON

Synagogues, Religion Classes, and Board Schools are within a few minutes' walk of the Estate.

SPLENDID POSITION NEAR PARKS AND OTHER OPEN SPACES.

TRAM FARES FROM SHOREDITCH ONE PENNY.

Apply for particulars at—

THE SUPERINTENDENT'S OFFICE, VICTORIA ROAD, STOKE NEWINGTON.

(Opposite West Hackney Church.)

Owners: The Four Per Cent. Industrial Dwellings Co., Ltd.

For a minority, entry was refused if they were suffering from an infectious disease, the two most common being favus, a scalp disease, and trachoma, a chronic eye disease. If rejected it could be traumatic. Often the father travelled alone and his wife came later. What if when his wife arrived with the children one child was refused entry? Should the mother return with all the children; or go back with the sick child and leave the others with the father; or let the sick child return alone? These were real problems faced by upwards of 1,000 immigrants.

The majority of those who arrived were transmigrants aiming to move on elsewhere, mainly to America. There was no compulsion on those who stayed to come to the East End, but they chose to do so to join relatives or friends already here or because it was an area in which they knew there were Jewish facilities to satisfy their needs – synagogues, kosher food, Jewish schools and work in the trades they knew – or simply because of a general desire to be among those with whom they felt most comfortable.

To quit the place they grew up in, to strike out for a distant seaport, taking steerage passage in what were often insanitary boats, for a country whose language they could not speak, and where most of them knew no one, meant it was the more enterprising and determined person, with a

TO THE GLORY OF GOD
AND IN
LOYAL AND PATRIOTIC MEMORY
OF THE SOLDIERS
OF THE JEWISH RACE AND FAITH
WHO LOST THEIR LIVES
IN THE SERVICE OF THEIR COUNTRY
DURING THE SOUTH AFRICAN WAR
1899-1902.

strong individualistic attitude, who was likely to be predominant among them. The immigrants brought with them only a little money – the majority arrived at the Port of London with 10 shillings or less a head – and a few tools of their trade. They brought with them harsh memories of oppression and economic deprivation, but they also brought with them hope and a determination to provide a better life for themselves and their families and to succeed in their newly adopted country.

Tablet outside the Central Synagogue in memory of Jewish soldiers who lost their lives during the Boer War (Courtesy The Jewish Historical Society of England)

The Shelter

If the arrivals were not met by someone who had a place to take them, there was one place they could turn to – the Poor Jews' Temporary Shelter. Simon Cohen, known as Simcha Becker, a recent immigrant who had not risen far above the level of poverty himself, maintained a rudimentary shelter at the rear of his bakery in Church Lane out of his own pocket. There the new arrivals could pray, study, sleep somehow and after a fashion be fed and even clothed. It was frowned upon by some of the community leaders, who had it closed down as insanitary. Following a public outcry against the closure, Hermann Landau, a Polish immigrant and stockbroker, the first Pole to be accepted into the Cousinhood, arranged for more sanitary accommodation at No.84 Leman Street, where new arrivals were allowed to stay for a maximum of 14 days and were given two meals a day while they found themselves other accommodation and began their search for work. Landau obtained money from the Rothschilds to fund it during its early days. It moved to Mansell Street in 1928 and to Brondesbury Park in 1973. It provided accommodation for between 1,000 and 4,000 immigrants and transmigrants a year, aiding them from the dockside until they boarded another ship or found a job or a place to live. The shelter sent representatives to meet the boats, and by 1900 had more or less

Ludwig Mond (1839–1909) came to England from Germany in 1862. He was co-founder of Brunner Mond & Co., one of the constituent firms that established Imperial Chemical Industries (ICI) in 1926.

eliminated the dockside pimps. Its meticulously kept records are today, under the guidance of Professor Aubrey Newman, being computerised and are throwing new light upon this period of Jewish immigration.

The established community and the newcomers

Fortunately for the newcomers, they did not enter a vacuum. As has been seen, by 1880 the community leaders had created a mini-welfare state with a network of efficient Jewish organisations that supplemented the general Poor Law system.

Further, in the 1880s the wealthier Jews mixed socially in influential Jewish and non-Jewish circles, even extending into royal circles. Several were members of the entourage of the Prince of Wales, later Edward VII. He liked the wealthy, and it did not matter to him whether a man's ancestors had come over with the Normans, or whether he had begun his career as a Hamburg bank clerk, particularly if he amused or informed the prince. If they happened to be Jewish, their religion was no bar. His so-called 'Marlborough House Set' included the Rothschilds, the Sassoons, Sir Ernest Cassel, Baron de Hirsch and the solicitor Sir George Lewis. Cassel was perhaps the king's closest male friend in his later years, and was so frequent a visitor that he became known as 'Windsor Cassel'. When Edward asked the Portuguese ambassador whether he had seen Oscar Wilde's *The Importance of being Earnest*, he said he had not, but he had seen the importance of being Ernest Cassel. (His grand-daughter Edwina married Lord Mountbatten of Burma). The Cousinhood's connections ensured that the community had a voice among the decision-makers.

The view was frequently expressed that three generations would have to pass before the foreign Jew became fully integrated into English society. Now the communal leaders were confronted by a completely new generation that had arrived, almost in an instant, and they were apprehensive that the machinery of relief they had set up would be overwhelmed. The lifeboat was full; they feared it would capsize with its passengers if more tried to clamber aboard.

They were also concerned that the newcomers, instantly recognizable by their different appearance, dress and language, who brought with them not only their bedding and their crockery but also their own way of life, might arouse and inflame anti-Semitism and be a destabilising element that could imperil both themselves and the established community. They engaged upon a triple strategy to deal with the problem: they attempted to dissuade any more

Sir Marcus Samuel, first Viscount Bearsted (1853–1927), founder of Shell Oil and Lord Mayor of London 1902–3. He financed the Jewish Maternity Home in Whitechapel (known as Mother Levy's). (Courtesy Guildhall Library, Corporation of London)

from coming; to integrate those who did come into English society; and finally to disperse them from the overcrowded East End.

In pursuance of the first objective, the Jewish Board of Guardians sent a message to its correspondents in Europe:

> In order to avoid trouble in the coming days we beseech every right thinking person among our brethren in Germany, Russia and Austria to place a barrier to the flow of foreigners, to persuade these voyagers not to venture to come to a land they do not know. It is better that they live a life of sorrow in their native place than bear the shame of famine and the disgrace of the missionaries, and perish in destitution in a strange land.

Even the Chief Rabbi lent his voice, and urged rabbis in eastern Europe to warn their congregants not to travel to England because, he told them, English charities could not cope, and difficulty in finding sufficient work was causing many men to violate the Sabbath and the holy days, and was driving them into the ensnaring net of the missionaries.

This first element of the strategy, preventing the emigrants from coming, failed – the immigrants continued to arrive. The Cousinhood then adopted the second part of their plan, integrating the immigrants into English life and society as quickly as possible. The *Jewish Chronicle* considered this to be a matter of the utmost urgency:

> The foreign poor form a community within the community. They come mostly from Poland; they, as it were, bring Poland with them, and they retain Poland while they stop here. This is most undesirable: it is more than a misfortune, it is a calamity. Our outside world is not capable of making minute discrimination between Jew and Jew, and forms its opinion of Jews in general as much, if not more, from them than from the Anglicized portion of the community. We are then responsible for them.

Two years later, in 1883, it warned that if the community did not deal speedily with the problem:

Sir Samuel Montagu (1832–1911), first Baron Swaythling and Liberal MP for Whitechapel 1885–1900. Founder of the Federation of Synagogues and a member of the Board of Guardians 1865–1883, he was also warden of the New West End Synagogue.

Lily Montagu (1873–1963), a daughter of Lord Swaythling. She was a co-founder in 1902, with Claude Montefiore, of the Jewish (Liberal) Religious Union, and the first woman in Jewish history to lead a religious movement. She later became the much-loved leader of the West Central Jewish Girls' Club.

Music Hall entertainments designed specially for the Jewish East End population were very popular

NO CHOOTSPERS ALLOWED
THE LAST NIGHT OF שבועות
AT THE
Green Dragon
Gardens, Stepney.
As Yontiff goes out, so, MIKE
SIMMONDS'
BENEFIT comes in !!
MONDAY, JUNE 13TH,
Masquerade Gala
CONCERT
Will be Supported by Choznnish sort of Singers.
Who Zing mit a *Dick-dse*, it's worth a *Penlisher Nadoonger* to hear 'em

A grand Shlanter Balloon,
In which the celebrated
Youpey, of Shoe Lane Will ascend accompanied by
the accomplished **Pysol** of antiquity **Michler.**
THE GARDENS
Have been **Clobered** up by very eminent **Howregim,**
and take my word it is **Zareshine.**
THE
NEW ORCHESTRA !
Auch has been **Gerpootzed** out, and **Shlooremized** by
the **Bolhose.**
A GROWSER PLOTZ
Which **Ousht fiel Gelt** will be erected
FOR DANCING.
In the course of the Evening an
Original Ballet, entitled **the Marshoogner Koler.**
In which **Phtcy** the **Phresser** and **Sorah,** the **Zouffer,**
Will sustain the principal characters introducing
A NEW WEAZEL DANCE.
Music by the Composer of 'Shlemezzle Can't be Perwented'.
PARUF HOPE VORRISHVOFFE
By **Mandler O'Lolly,** from the Staffordshire Potteries.
THE BALL ROOM
Solely for the admission of Ladies and Gentlemen in
Private Dress.
FIREWORKS, BY J. BROCK.
Admission to the whole Entertainments **6d.**
Tickets to be had at Mr Simmonds's Bookery Boyes, 7,
Cambridge Road, To commence at 5,
Carone, Printer, Hutchison Str. Middlesex St. Whitechapel.

An outcry will arise against the newly-come Hebrews which will react terribly upon the comfort and reputation of the older settlers. We owe it to our religion and to our brotherly feeling, we owe it to an enlightened view of self-interest, to deal promptly with the inflowing current from the turbid sea of Russian despair and degradation.

All sections of the community were urged to accept the newcomers and help as far as they could. When the Chief Rabbi Hermann Adler preached to a working-class congregation at Princelet Road Synagogue in March 1893 he impressed upon them what he considered the 'duty of the hour – your attitude, your obligations to brethren who have newly arrived here from the country where they have been so cruelly oppressed and so heartlessly persecuted'. He asked rhetorically:

Spitalfield Great Synagogue (Machzikei Hadass), on the corner of Fournier Street and Brick Lane. Erected in 1743 as a Huguenot Church, it became, in 1819, a Wesleyan Chapel, then a mission house for converting Jews, and in 1898 a synagogue. Today it is a mosque.

Shall we join the hue and cry which is raised in certain quarters and signify our assent to any measures that may prevent the immigration of 'destitute aliens' as they are called? ... No my brethren, emphatically no! Our conduct is clearly prescribed by the words of the Torah (Exodus 22:9).

'Thou shalt not oppress a stranger for ye know the heart of a stranger seeing that you were strangers in the land of Egypt'. Selfishness, lack of sympathy with those wretched outcasts is altogether unworthy of a human being. With us Jews it should be altogether unacceptable.

He reminded them that the time was not very distant when they themselves passed anxious lives within 'the inhospitable lands of the north'.

The crash course in integration

Every available resource – lay, ecclesiastical, educational and philanthropic – was mobilised for a crash course in the English language, Englishness, and patriotism. It must be emphasised that in engaging upon this task of encouraging the immigrant to adopt English ways neither the schools nor the community leaders required any sacrifice of religious beliefs on their part; they did not encourage religious assimilation. On the contrary, the Jewish schools were key to preserving Jewish identity. Integration was the object, and pride in being Jewish was promoted to the fullest extent. Baron Ferdinand de Rothschild told the children of Stepney Jewish Schools, 'never forget so long as you live that you are Jews and Jewesses', and the aim of the highly acculturated Jewish elite was to create patriotic Britons who preserved their Jewish history, tradition and beliefs.

The schools, Jewish and non-Jewish, were the main vehicles for integration. Before 1870 it was the Jewish voluntary charity schools, largely funded by the Jewish elite families, particularly the Rothschilds, that bore the brunt of the task. The Jews' Free School in Bell Lane led the way. The Revd Simeon Singer, whose Prayer Book is still widely used today, described the work carried out there as a 'veritable redemption'.

The Hampstead Synagogue choir, c.1900. A mixed choir sang at regular services from the first Sabbath that the synagogue opened, despite the Chief Rabbi having expressed reservations.

Opposite page: Pupils of the Jews' Free School on arrival at the school and before leaving.

If one could photograph the mental features and spiritual condition of most of the children when they entered and again when they left, it would be no easy matter to recognise them; so complete is the transformation. It is little short of a marvel that, from material apparently so unpromising, educational results so extraordinary are produced.

The *Jewish Chronicle* boasted that a young Pole could be placed in the Jews' Free School with the assurance that at the end of his training he would be turned out a young Englishman. The Board of Trade Report of 1894 into the effects of immigration was a little more circumspect, noting that immigrant children emerged from JFS *almost* indistinguishable from English children.

Between 1880 and 1900, one-third of all London's Jewish children passed through its doors. Many were foreign born, and arrived unable to speak English. The school taught them English from day one, provided them with a refuge and a means of escape from poverty, educated them in both secular and religious studies, anglicized them and sent them out in the world fit to integrate into society.

Moses Angel, the remarkable headteacher at the school for 55 years, also the first editor of the *Jewish Chronicle*, helped to create a school so famous and successful that even Tsar Nicholas I made a donation to its funds. When it was difficult for a religious Jew to obtain teacher training experience, the school operated as a teachers' training college, providing qualified teachers for almost every Jewish school in the British Empire and more recruits for the Jewish ministry than Jews' College, which was established specifically for that purpose. The members of the Rothschild family were its most devoted supporters, and the school's logo and uniform still carry the Rothschild colours of gold and blue.

Among the school's most colourful alumni were Barney Barnato (1852–97), the extravagant, larger-than-life financier who went from rags to riches and back again after amalgamating his diamond company with Cecil Rhodes's De Beers Company, and General Morris ('Two Gun') Cohen, the son of an East End tailor who left the Jews' Free School to attend a Jewish reform school and became a general in the Chinese army serving under Sun Yat-Sen and Chiang Kai-shek. Samuel Gompers, the first

Moses Angel (1819–98), first joint editor of the Jewish Chronicle, *was headmaster of the Jews' Free School in Whitechapel for 55 years from 1842.*

President of the American Federation of Labor, was also a pupil at the school.

In addition to the Jews' Free School there were the Jews' Infant Schools in Commercial Street and Buckle Street, and the Sephardi Gates of Hope School in Thrawl Street. The Stepney Jewish Schools in Stepney Green were the most native in pupil composition; at the turn of the century only four percent of its pupils were born abroad. There were the Westminster Jews' Free School in Hanway Place off Tottenham Court Road; the Bayswater Jewish School, later known as the Solomon Wolfson School, which had opened in 1866; and the Borough School, south of the Thames, founded in 1867, which attracted pupils from Walworth, Southwark, Bermondsey, Brixton, Clapham and Lambeth. In 1870 they were all well-managed and some had to turn away pupils for lack of space.

A sketch in the Daily Graphic *of a class in the Jews' Free School, 1895.*

The 1870 Education Act paved the way for the provision of state schools and compulsory education. The London School Board took to its task enthusiastically and efficiently. Before it was taken over by the London County Council in 1904 it had built 469 schools, of which 78 were in the East End. Its first school, in Old Castle Street, was state-of-the-art and could accommodate 1,250 pupils. It was expected that the local Jewish children would flock to register, particularly those who could not obtain a place at JFS. To the surprise and consternation of the School Board it attracted less than 100 children in the first few months. The immigrant Jewish parents, having endured the restrictions on Jewish education in Russia and Poland, brought with them a jaundiced view of state officialdom, and feared that Board schools might be missionary in nature. They were prepared to suffer hardship once more rather than surrender their children into the hands of the State.

The solution to the problem was supplied by Moses Angel. He advised the Board to appoint a Jewish headmaster, and recommended Abraham Levy, a former pupil of his who was currently headmaster of the Gates of Hope School. Recently married, Levy had to interrupt his honeymoon to take up the

Bethnal Green Great Synagogue. This building suffered heavy bomb damage in World War Two and was completely rebuilt. (Courtesy Tower Hamlets Local History Library and Archives)

post. Almost immediately Jewish children began registering. Jewish holidays were observed, and during the winter months classes were dismissed at 2pm on Fridays so that pupils could prepare for the Sabbath. To all intents and purposes, Old Castle Street became a 'Jewish' school within the state education system, although Levy made it clear that he would not tamper in the slightest degree with the religion of the non-Jewish children in his care. Within a few years the school had nearly 1,500 pupils, 95 percent of whom were Jewish, and it was used as a model for persuading the immigrants to send their children to other Board Schools.

By the turn of the century there were 16 'Jewish' Board schools in the East End, including those in Berner Street, Buck's Row, Chicksand Street, Deal Street, Gravel Lane and Settle Street. They held Jewish prayers, had a timetable

An artist's impression of the West Hampstead Synagogue that opened in 1902.

The entrance to the East London Synagogue in Rectory Square. It attracted members because its marriage fees were low.

Spital Square Poltava Synagogue, c.1920, one of the many synagogues named after the town from which its founders originated. (Courtesy Tower Hamlets Local History Library and Archives)

geared to the Jewish religious calendar, and outside school hours Jewish religious classes were held by the Jewish Religious Education Board (JREB) on the school premises. As time passed the state schools were more frequently used. In 1886, Jewish schools catered for 63 percent of all of London's Jewish pupils. In 1894 the figure was 49 percent, in 1900 37 percent, and in 1911 only 20 percent. No new Jewish schools were established in London until the 1930s.

Giving evidence to the Royal Commission on Alien Immigration in 1902, Joseph Rowden, the non-Jewish headmaster of Deal Street School, said:

My first classes contain 175 boys ... almost all of whom were born abroad or have parents born abroad. Notwithstanding this fact, the lads have become thoroughly English. They have acquired our language. They take a keen and intelligent interest in all that concerns the welfare of our country ... they enter heartily into English games ... Jewish lads who pass through our schools will grow up to be intelligent, industrious, temperate and law-abiding citizens and ... will add to the wealth and stability of the British Empire.

There were special classes in English for adults. Some parents tried to catch up with their children and made strenuous efforts to improve their English and adapt themselves to their new homeland. In 1894 there were nearly 500 pupils a night attending the Russo-Jewish Committee's free adult classes in English. Observers were impressed by their zeal. There was a report in

Artillery Lane Synagogue, one of the Federation Synagogues. (Courtesy Tower Hamlets Local History Library and Archives)

the *Daily Chronicle*, in 1908.

I would like to take your readers to some of our ghetto evening schools, the schools where the adult Russian and German Jews, artificially thrust back into darkness by European governments, clutch at their last hope of knowledge. They come to this country like their children ignorant of the English language, very often unable to read, write or add up. They are at work all day ... very often doubled up in some little sweating den. In the evening they rush from their work with scarcely a bite for food straight to our evening classes ... in a few months they will learn to read or write our English tongues almost as well as the Christian workman who has forgotten half he has learned at school. I never feel prouder of England than when standing in these schools and watching this work ... nothing is more pathetic than the desire of these people to be English, to work for England, fight for England. England is the only western European nation that has been wholly just to the Jews and in return England is the only country where the Jew is as proud of his nation as of his race.

Congregation of Jacob. A Federation Synagogue in Commercial Road.

Where they lived and housing conditions

The top priorities of the new arrivals were to find accommodation and then work. Their chosen area, the two square miles of the East End, was already one of the most densely populated in England, and worsening because of extensive slum clearance operations and the razing of several streets to provide room for the extension of the railway.

In Whitechapel in 1871 there were an average of nine inhabitants per house;

by 1901 it was 14. The definition of the Medical Officer of Health for London
that more than two people per room constituted overcrowding, meant that 85
percent of all housing in Whitechapel was overcrowded. The ratio was even
higher in some dwellings. With one or more lodgers, several children, perhaps
grandparents and other relatives, almost every Jewish immigrant household
was cramped. It was not uncommon for eight or nine individuals to share two
small rooms, with children sleeping head-to-toe, three or four to a bed.

Rooms were let out at 5s per week, which in turn were partitioned for
subletting to a lodger for 1s per week. 'Give a Jew an inch', their opponents
said, 'and he will put a bed in it; give him two, and he will take in a lodger'.
It was in the neighbourhood of Old Montague Street, Booth Street, Hanbury
Street and Chicksand Street that some of the worst cases of insanitary accommodation and overcrowding were found. Further, many private houses
doubled as workshops. The *Lancet* carried out a special investigation and
reported in 1884 that:

> In Emily Place ... *we found five persons living in one room, while in*

another house we came upon a Jewish potato dealer who kept his wife, five children and a huge stock of potatoes all in one room measuring five yards by six yards. There was one bed in the room and probably some of the family slept on the floor.

In Hanbury Street we found eighteen workers crowded in a small room measuring eight yards by four yards and a half, and not quite eight feet high. The first two floors of this house were let out to lodgers who were also Jews ... their rooms were clean but damp as water was coming through the rotting wall ... the sink was not trapped, the kitchen range was falling to pieces, while the closet was a permanent source of trouble. A flushing apparatus had been provided but this discharged water outside the pan; the water consequently came out under the seat and flowed across the yard to the wall opposite, which was eaten away at its base ... the top room ... had at times to hold eighteen persons, working in the heat of the gas and the stove, warming the pressing irons, surrounded by mounds of dust and chips from the cut cloth, breathing an atmosphere full of woollen particles containing more or less injurious dyes. It is not surprising that so large a proportion of working tailors break down from diseases of the respiratory organs.

As a result of overcrowding, a large part of home life was lived out of doors. The more elderly sat in their doorways and enjoyed the passing scene and chatted with relatives and friends, adolescents searched for excitement, and the streets were the children's playground.

The Jewish community did its best to combat overcrowding. The work of the Jewish Board of Guardians' Sanitary Committee has already been mentioned. According to the *Jewish Chronicle*, in 1884 Baroness Charlotte de Rothschild, Lord Rothschild's mother, who was on her deathbed, urged him to devote his energies to improving the housing of the workers. In 1885, the Four Per Cent Industrial Dwelling Company, of which Lord Rothschild was the chairman, was incorporated. Its aim was 'To provide the industrial classes with more commodious and healthy lodgings and dwellings than those they now inhabit, giving them the maximum of accommodation for a minimum rent compatible with the yielding of a net four per cent per annum dividend on the paid up capital of the company'. The interest rate was deliberately pitched lower than that aimed at by other housing organisations.

Other blocks, such as the Peabody Buildings, charged 7s to 8s per week rent, a sum beyond the means of the average Jewish immigrant. In the first Rothschild Buildings, opened in Flower and Dean Street in 1887, the rent was just 2s 6d for a single room, 4s 6d for two rooms and joint scullery, 5s for two rooms and own scullery, 5s 6d for three rooms and joint scullery, and 7s 6d for three rooms and own scullery. Others followed in Thrawl Street, Brady Street and Stepney Green. By 1901 they housed 4,600 people. The *Jewish Chronicle* claimed that 'among the many religious bodies working among the poor the Jewish community can lay claim to be the only one that has taken upon itself, in a practical manner, the housing of the poor. Whilst other religious bodies have conferred, the Jewish community has acted'.

The influx caused the East End Jewish population to burst out of the confines between Aldgate and Commercial Street. It pushed east past Brick Lane into Mile End, north past Hanbury Street to the fringes of Bethnal Green, and south across Whitechapel Road and Commercial Road as far as Cable Street. Beyond this a solid body of Irish impeded further progress. The Russell and Lewis map in *The Jew in London* (see pages 8-9) showed that by 1900 some streets to the north of Whitechapel, such as Wentworth Street, Old

Montague Street, Flower and Dean Street and Fashion Street, and to the south Plumbers Row, Scarborough Street and Providence Row, were almost 100 percent in Jewish occupation, and many others had more than 75 percent penetration.

Despite the high-density occupation, the housing was not all bad news. True, some of the housing in and around Brady Street and Old Montague Street and in the dozens of little surrounding courts and alleys was in poor condition, and bugs abounded and were a perennial problem. But even though shabbily furnished, and even though there might not be enough beds for all who had to live there, the Jewish mothers worked constantly to keep their homes clean and welcoming – and they succeeded.

Sketch of a missionary seeking converts, 1910.

Amid the small, basic, closely huddled two-ups and two-downs in the narrow streets and alleys, there were also 'houses of sunken eminence once inhabited by well paid skilled workers or even by the merchant classes who had moved elsewhere as the neighbourhood slowly declined'. The new blocks of buildings erected in the 1880s and 1890s in such as Flower and Dean Street, though not things of beauty, were sanitary, and had a safe courtyard in which the children could play. Streets such as Fashion Street or New Road boasted houses with high ceilings, and Mansell Street, Leman Street and Great Prescott Street still contained the homes of some of the socially and communally prominent families.

Many of the families were, of course, separated, with husbands in England waiting to send for their families, or the family here and the father in the United States waiting to save enough money to send for them. Consequently uncles often replaced fathers, and cousins became as brothers and sisters. Neighbours had a near family relationship with each other.

Jack the Ripper

There is nothing like a sensational murder to put a place on the map; to have five within the space of 10 weeks attracts international notoriety. All took place between 31 August and 9 November 1888 in the heart of the Jewish East End quarter. The eyes of the world concentrated on the many dark cobbled alleyways and narrow streets of Whitechapel that provided an ideal setting for the murderer.

The victims, all women and mostly prostitutes, had their throats cut from ear to ear, the lower parts of their abdomens completely ripped open, and their bowels left protruding, in one case with intestines strewn all over the street. Polly Nicholls met her fate on 31 August at Bucks Row (now Durward Street); Anna Chapman on 8 September in Hanbury Street; Elizabeth Stride and Catherine Eddowes, both on 30 September at Berner Street and Mitre Street respectively; and Mary Kelly at Millers Court off Dorset Street on 9 November. The Jewish community would have known some of them, for Polly Nicholls lived in Thrawl Street, Elizabeth Stride in lodgings in Flower and Dean Street, and Mary Kelly in Loleworth Street.

The fear aroused, and the search to find someone to blame, knew no bounds. Within days of the first murder the finger was pointed at the Jewish community. The *East London Observer* reported that:

> *On Saturday in several quarters of East London the crowds who assembled in the streets began to assume a very threatening attitude towards the Hebrew population of the district. It was repeatedly asserted that no Englishman could have perpetrated such a horrible crime as that of Hanbury Street, and that it must have been done by a Jew – and forthwith the crowds began to threaten and abuse such of the unfortunate Hebrews as they found in the streets. Happily the presence of a large number of police prevented a riot actually taking place.*

The Central News Agency received a letter postmarked 28 September in which the writer referred to the first two murders in a grisly and jocular way and signed himself 'Jack the Ripper'. A postcard received two days later read, 'You'll hear about Saucy Jack's work tomorrow. Double event this time', and indeed the third and fourth murders followed.

REAR OF NO 29, HANBURY S

O 29, HANBURY ST

M. A. RICHARDSON
ROUGH PACKING
CASE MAKER

⊕ WHERE BODY
WAS FO

ANOTHER
MURDER
IN
WHITECHAPEL
ARREST

Scene at the site of Jack the Ripper's Hanbury Street victim, Anna Chapman.

MILLERS COURT

ENTRANCE TO MILLERS COURT IN DORSET STRE

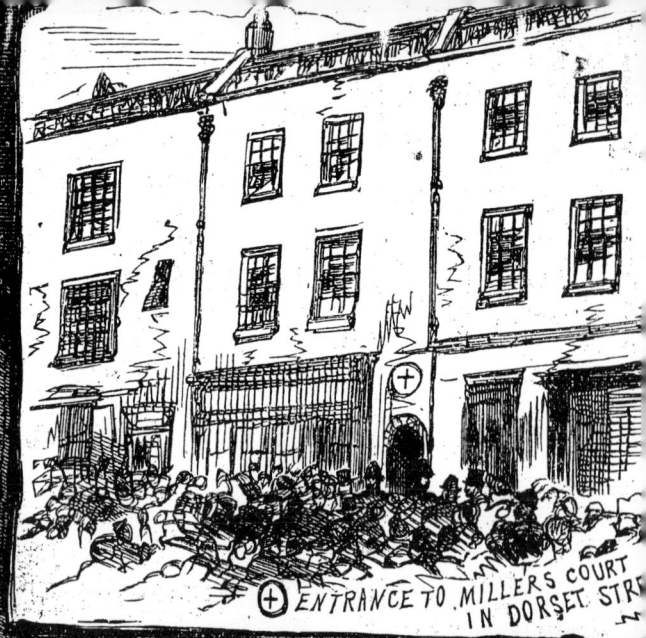

Jack the Ripper's last victim was Mary Kelly, murdered in Millers Court, Dorset Street

IT WAS THROUGH THE BROKEN PANES OF THIS WINDOW THAT THE BODY THE MURDERED WOMAN WAS FIRST SEEN

I'm not a butcher,
I'm not a Yid,
Nor yet a foreign skipper,
But I'm your own high-hearted friend,
Yours truly
Jack the Ripper.

The injuries were such that it was believed that the murderer must either have had a medical background or be a butcher. Suspicion fell upon doctors and then on *shochetim*, Jewish ritual slaughterers, and two were arrested but both had perfect alibis. The police looked elsewhere when the City Divisional Surgeon examined knives commonly used by *shochetim* and concluded that they could not have been used in any of the murders as they were single-edged and not pointed, whereas the mutilations on all the victims indicated a pointed blade.

Following further leads the police issued a description of a man they were seeking: 'Age 37, height, 5ft 8in. Rather dark beard and moustache; dark jacket, dark vest and trousers, black scarf and black felt hat. Speaks with foreign accent.' It was a description that

34–37 Stepney Green. The home of the Jewish Workhouse from 1876–1907.

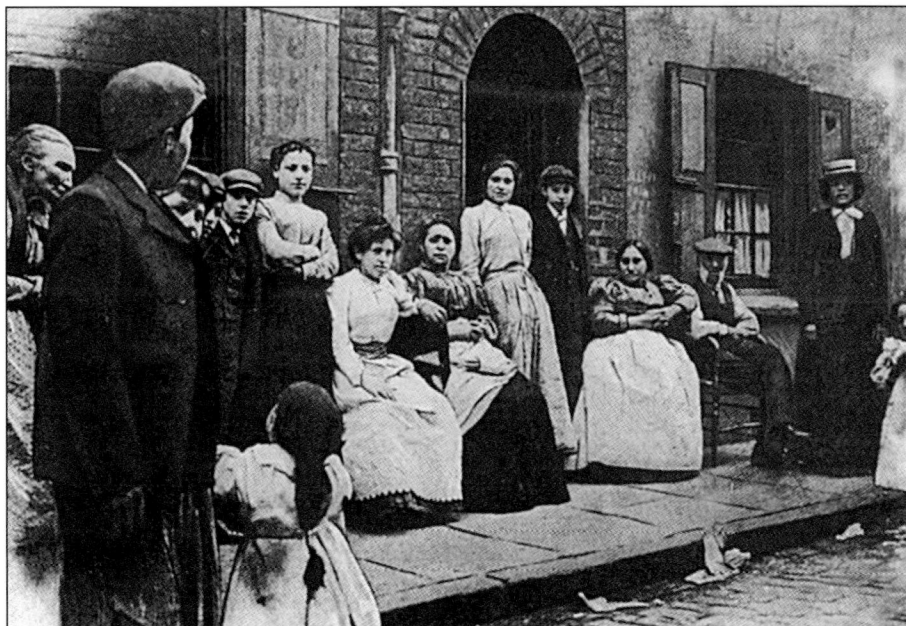

The crowded housing conditions led people to sit outside as often as possible, 1900.

A sketch of Whitechapel High Street in 1901.

could have fitted half the male Jews living in the district and led to several innocents being picked up for questioning.

The mystery has never been solved and every year brings yet another book embracing another theory and another suspect. These have ranged from HRH Prince Albert Victor, to the Duke of Clarence, a tramp living in a workhouse and a Russian anarchist. One benefit came from Jack's activities: the murders drew attention to a deprived area and galvanised efforts to rid the East End of the worst of its slums and alleyways.

Work

The immigrants wasted no time in getting work, usually supporting themselves from the day they arrived. They were diligent and willing to work long hours. Beatrice Potter said 'the Jew will accept the lowest terms rather than remain out of employment'. The tension of adjustment in a new land, the insecurity of seasonal work, the desire to bring over members of one's family or save up the steamship fare to America, all made their contribution to the Jewish worker's desire to work hard. He did not regard himself as one with a fixed station in life and had the desire to be an entrepreneur even though the earn-

*Tailors' workshop,
c.1916. Crowded
conditions and long
hours. (Courtesy Tower
Hamlets Local History
Library and Archives)*

ings of the masters were often not much higher than the wages they paid their employees.

In a new country and among natives who were more securely established in their trades, the Jew's unlimited application to work was unwelcome, the more so because of the grounds for believing he undercut native English workers. They were accused at the Trade Union Congress of 1894 of working 15 hours a day 'on cold coffee and bread and cheese, and although they do not seem to earn any wages they often in a short time are able to set up in business for themselves (laughter)'.

During the 1881–1914 period, two-thirds of all English Jews were engaged in just three, mainly seasonal trades – tailoring, shoemaking and furniture making – that could be operated in improvised premises (in part of a house, in a shed, or in a disused building).

The invention of the Singer sewing machine in the 1850s revolutionised the clothing industry. Ready-made clothing

*A socialist cartoon
porteraying an over-
worked tailor and an
exploitative employer.*

An interior view of the premises of Messrs Moses & Son, tailors, Minories c.1847. (By courtesy of the Guildhall Library, Corporation of London)

eventually rose to dominate the clothing market against the wishes of the traditional English tailor. Durable inexpensive clothes of presentable quality and appearance were a phenomenon of the 1840s and 1850s and one that became intimately bound up with the Jewish entrepreneurs.

In 1860, E. Moses & Son boasted that it was 'the first house in London or may we say in the world that established the system of new clothing ready made. Eighty percent of the population purchased ready made clothing because the prejudice against it had been conquered by the reputation of our firm. Thousands of tailors have followed our example, but we continue in the van'. All of Moses's shops were closed on the Sabbath. Later Montague Burton, a Russian immigrant, founded the well-known chain of tailoring shops.

In the 1880s and succeeding decades tailoring was the occupation of more than half of all Jewish working men and women. Certain aspects of tailoring were considered 'Jewish', such as pressing, buttonhole making and machining. Basting and felling employed young girls or women. Newcomers in the trade earned only

In 1889 the tailors won the right to a 12-hour working day.

NOTICE

to

TAILORS & TAILORESSES !

As the employees of

MESSERS HEBBERT & Co.,

35 & 37, Bethnal Green Rd., E.

are on

STRIKE,

All Workers belonging to the Tailoring trade are requested to

KEEP AWAY from that place.

Tailors' Strike Committee

"White Hart," Greenfield Str.
Commercial Rd., E.

Worker's Friend Printing Office, 40, Berner St., Commercial Rd. E.

a few shillings a week, lived on the proverbial herrings, and slept on the floor. After about a year a general hand earned a pound a week, middle grades £1 to £1 10s; a skilled worker £2 to £2 10s. It was rare before 1914 for a Jew to reach the topmost level of skill, that of a cutter or patternmaker, and the Jewish workshop usually received its work already cut.

For many the working conditions were dreadful, with long hours, cramped conditions, little ventilation and dangerous tools. Because of the seasonal nature of so many of the Jewish trades, workers found themselves beginning at dawn and working halfway through the night to get out orders, followed by a period when they earned only intermittently.

When Jewish tailors went on strike in 1889 they were seeking a 12-hour day: an hour off for dinner; half an hour for tea; and no homework after working hours. And that was for a six-day week.

'Sweating' was the word used to describe the cramped workshops unregulated by factory legislation, in which long hours were worked by both master and employees in extremely unsanitary conditions. The Jews were widely blamed for introducing the system. During the late 1880s an anti-sweating movement spread and a House of Lords Select Committee enquired into the matter. It concluded:

An East End Sunday market (Courtesy Tower Hamlets Local History Library and Archives)

Whitechapel Art Gallery and the adjacent library 1905, which both contributed to the education and advancement of the East End Jews, children and adults alike. (Courtesy Tower Hamlets Local History Library and Archives)

We are of the opinion that certain trades are, to some extent, affected by the presence of poor foreigners, for the most part Russian and Polish Jews. These Jews are not charged with immorality or with vice of any description, though represented by some witnesses as being uncleanly in their persons and habits. On the contrary, they are represented on all hands as thrifty and industrious, and they seldom or never come on the rates, as the Jews support by voluntary contributions all their indigent members. What is shown is that the Jewish immigrants can live on what would be starvation wages to Englishmen, that they work for a number of hours almost incredible in length, and that until of late they have not easily lent themselves to trade combinations.

Advertisement in the Jewish Year Book of 1898 for E. Barnett & Co. Note its telegram address.

A view of 164–167 Aldersgate Street showing the premises of Harrison's the pawnbrokers; G. Harrison, picture frame makers; and Woolf & Hyman furriers. (Courtesy Guildhall Library, Corporation of London)

The major conclusion was that sweating was far from a Jewish monopoly, although it had become unfairly associated with them. It was clearly demonstrated that it had existed before the Jews came, and existed in trades in which no Jews were engaged.

Cabinetmaking

Furniture making began in the East End in the first half of the 19th century. Based in the Curtain Road and Old Street area of Shoreditch, it had by 1870 outstripped the West End as London's main furniture producing area. It was characterised by small workshops established with little capital investment, low wages, long hours, subdivision of labour and subcontracting.

Many post-1880 Jewish immigrants arrived with cabinet-making skills in every field of domestic furniture, from general carpenters to specialist wood-turners, carvers and marquetry workers. They found work fairly easily, and the trade was so broken down into small compartments that complete 'greeners' could find some position for a minimal wage and had an opportunity to learn a trade. Some firms allowed them to sleep on the workshop floor until they found their own accommodation. The Board of Guardians did its best to obtain apprenticeships in the trade for school leavers.

At that time there was little machinery involved in the trade and it was easier, even than in tailoring to start up a business on one's own account. A Booth survey reporter noted that 'a pound's worth of tools and a second

1901: an East End 'schnorrer' (beggar).

Aldgate in 1914. (Courtesy Tower Hamlets Local History Library and Archives)

pound in cash starts many a cabinet maker on a career as an independent worker, and double that amount will often convert him into an employer'.

In the 1920s the hub of the business was still in Curtain Road and Old Street, but had also spread into Great Eastern Street, Hackney Road, Bethnal Green, Stoke Newington, Clapton and Stepney. There were at least 23 Jewish-owned workshops in Brick Lane alone, 19 in Columbia Road, 13 in Gibraltar Walk, 17 in Kingsland Road and 14 in Virginia Road. Many operated in the top part of their houses.

One or two outgrew the space available in the East End. Louis Lebus, who had arrived in the 1840s, started with a workshop in Whitechapel. On his death in 1879 his son Harris took over the business and moved into multistorey premises in Tabernacle Street in Shoreditch. By 1899 the firm had 1,000 employees, mostly immigrants. It claimed to be the largest cabinet manufacturer in the country and moved out to Tottenham to a 40-acre site. Two other large immigrant concerns, Flatau the boot and shoemakers and Gestetners the duplicating process company, joined them there. Their factories became a magnet for Jewish immigration and it became a predominantly lower middle and working-class area. A few went there under the Dispersal Committee Scheme and by 1905 there were an estimated 2,000 Jews living in the area.

In the inter-war years the cheaper end of the furniture market broadened when there was an increase in the number of new houses built for lower and upper middle-class working families. New materials such as plywood came into use and larger firms began to mechanise production. Three-piece suites and bedroom suites made their appearance. Many firms moved out to the Lea Valley area where land was cheap, there was space for expansion and the river provided an additional means of transport of goods.

Several Jewish cabinet makers with East End immigrant beginnings became household names. In addition to Harris Lebus there was Beautility, founded by Simon Sadovsky in 1896 in Shoreditch; Hille started by Salamon Hille in Bethnal Green; Austinsuite, the company of Frank Austin and his three brothers, the sons of a bamboo furniture maker; and Ducal, today a major producer of pine furniture, founded by Sydney Wiseman in Ducal Street, E2. H. & I. Epstein was started by Morris Epstein, who arrived from Russia in 1890 and opened his workshop in Gun Street in 1913. Two of his sons founded H. & I. Epstein in Hanbury Street in 1950 and became well-known as suppliers to affluent Jewish families.

Jews were also well represented in the timber merchant trade in Eastern Europe, and there were several Jewish timber merchants in London.

Tobacco

Tobacco was one of the earliest trades traditionally associated with the Dutch Jews who formed the main body of Jewish immigrants in the middle of the 19th century. At that time, when there were three times as many Dutch as Polish Jews in the Whitechapel and St George's area, cigar making was the major Jewish occupation, with tailoring way behind. However, cigar making was less prominent among Eastern European Jewish occupations.

The firm of Godfrey Phillips began in the 1840s, as did the immigrant family business of Salmon & Gluckstein, which opened a factory in Soho and moved to Whitechapel in the following decade. It operated a chain of 140 tobacconist shops before selling out in 1902.

Until 1883 cigarettes were made by hand, but in that year an American invented a cigarette-making machine that revolutionised the business. Wills of Bristol acquired the British rights to it and dominated the trade. The Russian-born Jew, Bernhard Baron, whose family had emigrated to America, patented another machine and came to England to exploit it. He purchased the old-established firm of Carreras and expanded the business greatly. He became a multi-millionaire, and a philanthropist on a grand scale, but during his first

The Queen's Hall in the People's Palace in Mile End Road, c.1900. Opened by Queen Victoria in 1887 as an educational and leisure centre it was much used and appreciated by the East End community (Courtesy Tower Hamlets Local History Library and Archives)

five years struggled financially. Speaking of that period he said, 'I worked hard,
worked always, took no interest in anything outside my work.' It was not until
the sixth year that he made a profit. In the 1920s he had the popular Black
Cat and Craven A brands. Other smaller Jewish companies, Abdullah,
Marcovitch and Cohen Weenen, J. Wix and Sons and Ardath, also had popular brands. Rothman's of Pall Mall was founded in the late 19th century by
Louis Rothman, who sold cigarettes from his Pall Mall shop by mail order to
embassies and various British institutions overseas.

Boots and shoes

Trades in which the small workshops could no longer compete with the new factories with their improved machinery and equipment led to the irresistible decline of several of the immigrant trades. Boot and shoemaking illustrated the classic transition from domestic and outwork production to factory production. In season, work started at dawn and continued till halfway through the night. When trade was slack, work and wages were only intermittent. In the early 1890s a newly-invented riveting machine superseded the need for skilled lasters, and by 1901 there were only 149 bootmaking workshops in Stepney compared to 1,300 in the garment trades. Fifteen years earlier there had been equal numbers.

The situation of the Jewish shoemaker-entrepreneur and his team steadily worsened. The small employers were as helpless as their workers against seasonal fluctuation and could do nothing to maintain the price they might extract from a wholesale house for their work. The sons of the original immigrants did not take to the boot and shoe trade at all.

The Brady Boys' Club in Durward Street, founded in 1896. (Courtesy Tower Hamlets Local History Library and Archives)

Slipper making, cap making and furriers

Slipper making had a brief surge upwards in the 1890s. Displaced shoe lasters turned to sewing slippers of poorer quality, but the trade did not last long. Cap making, as distinct from hat making, was a trade practically created by the Jews and it grew to some importance. In 1890 there were 120 small workshops in the East End. Once again it was an operation that broke down each step of the process so that comparatively unskilled work was required at each stage. Furriers' work stood at a fairly low level of skill. Cheap capes and dyed rabbit skins were made in imitation of more expensive furs, but it too was an unhealthy occupation, conducted in cramped, poorly ventilated conditions.

Other Jewish occupations were iron and tin plate makers, brush makers, cardboard box makers, house painters and decorators, butchers, poulterers, bakers and of course small shopkeepers.

Trade unions

The immigrant worker was not good material for trade unionism. In Russia and Poland they had no experience of trade unionism along English lines. They were too individualistic in their outlook, too fractious, were largely employed in small workshops that did not readily lend themselves to unionisation, and in any event aspired to be employers themselves. The seasonal nature of their work and the necessarily irregular hours made the fixing of regular hours and conditions almost impracticable.

One trade unionist said, more in hope than expectation, 'the self-assertive individualistic Jews will learn that mutual recriminations are not the principal object of committee and general meetings'. The *Ladies Garment Worker* said in 1910 that the Jews had tried every sort of union, 'independent unions, international unions, amalgamated unions, syndicalist unions, social democratic and anarchistic unions, pure and simple and Sabbath observing unions. But to introduce higher fees and various benefits, to amass a large treasury, to avoid strikes as far as possible, to learn the methods of the powerful English unions – this they have not tried.' In England as a whole trade unions of this period were building up their strength, but this was not mirrored by the Jewish unions.

From the end of the 1880s to the first decade of the 20th century there was a constant rise and fall, formation and dissolution, fission and reunion of small Jewish unions in the tailoring trade and a similar experience in the boot and shoe trade. It must be said that although there was an element of success in the provinces, particularly in Leeds, the trade union movement made no real headway in London with the Jewish workers.

Throughout the 1880s and the 1930s there was a maze of unstable small firms in the East End, with enterprises constantly going under and new ones opening. There were many failures but success stories too. Some major undertakings had been founded by the earlier settlers, for example ICI, of which Sir Alfred Mond became the first chairman. Hugo Hirst prospered in the electrical industry with GEC. In commerce, Marcus Samuel and his brother built up the Shell Oil Company.

Then the eastern newcomers began to contribute major enterprises whose outlets could be found throughout London. Michael Marks, who had emigrated from Russian Poland in 1882, was one of the founders of Marks & Spencer and had 36 stores by 1900. Jack Cohen, the creator of Tesco, was born in Rutland Street in 1898, the son of a Polish Jewish tailor. He joined his father as an apprentice tailor, served in the Royal Flying Corps during World War One, and used his £30 gratuity to buy supplies of surplus NAAFI foodstuffs that he sold from a market stall in Hackney. He established the Tesco trade name, opened shops, and by 1939 had 100 outlets, almost all in London. Following a visit to the United States after World War Two he pioneered the self-service system in England, and Tesco now has shops nationwide. Salmon & Gluckstein moved into the catering trade in 1887, and the brothers Montague and Isidore Gluckstein, their cousin Alfred Salmon and Joseph Lyons opened the famous Lyons tea shops. By 1914 there were 200 of them, designed for clerks and lady shoppers, providing cheap food. In 1896 the company opened the Trocadero in Piccadilly for the needs of the wealthy, and the first of its much-loved and much-missed Corner Houses was opened in 1909.

Whitechapel Road in 1932. (Courtesy Tower Hamlets Local History Library and Archives)

The Alien Issue

From 1881 to 1905 the 'alien issue' posed a serious problem, one that was accentuated because the concentration of Jews in small areas of London and the provinces made it appear that they were more numerous than they actually were. Everything about them was different: their language, their garb, their side-curls and non-drinking habits. As a result they stood out. Suddenly, in the eyes of the general population, they were everywhere, millions of them, or so it seemed. In 1892, *Whitaker's Almanac* claimed that Jews were pouring in at the rate of about 140,000 a year when the true figure was about 4,000, while another source calculated that by 1910 there would be over seven million Jews in the country. There were in fact less than a quarter of a million at that date.

There was a widespread feeling in Britain that some provision for restricting immigration was necessary. Among those leading the opposition to immigration were Arnold White and Major William Gordon Evans, the Member of Parliament for Stepney. Arnold White, a proclaimed anti-Semite, warned against the 'sinister consequences of Jewish immigration' and forecast that national life would be stifled. There were warnings of riots, which never took place.

Everyone knew that when politicians and others spoke of 'aliens' they meant Eastern European Jews. In February 1902 the *Pall Mall Gazette* fulminated against 'the filth, insolence, and depravity of this refuse of Europe which is being dumped at our doors'. Complaints were made that they arrived destitute and dirty, spread diseases and were a burden on the rates; that several of them were criminals, anarchists and immoral persons; that their concentration in one area led to increased rents, to the payment of key-money, and the driving out of the original inhabitants; that they did not assimilate, and in some areas interfered with the observance of the Christian Sunday. The last quarter of the 19th century was a period of economic depression, and it was said that the immigrants provided a pool of cheap labour and depressed wages, and that they dealt only with fellow Jews so that non-Jewish trade suffered. All these complaints were investigated, and with the exception of the allegation about bringing about an increase in rents, were proved to be either unfounded or greatly exaggerated.

A Royal Commission, of which Lord Rothschild was a member, was appointed in 1902 to consider the matter. Several prominent Jewish witnesses appeared before the Commission to support the immigrants' case, including Sir Samuel Montagu, Theodor Herzl, and Leopold Greenberg of the English Zionist Federation, later editor of the *Jewish Chronicle*. The Royal Commission concluded that there was no case for the total exclusion of alien immigrants, but five of the seven members thought that there was a case for powers to be introduced to regulate the flow, particularly from Eastern Europe, to prevent overcrowding, and that power should be provided to deport 'undesirables', defined as criminals, prostitutes, idiots, persons of bad character and others likely to become a charge on public funds. Lord Rothschild opposed restriction of any kind.

The remarkable scene in Sydney Street, Stepney, in 1911, when the Scots Guards and the Royal Horse Artillery, under the command of the then Home Secretary, Winston Churchill, were called out to deal with two suspected anarchist murderers of three police officers (Courtesy Tower Hamlets Local History Library and Archives)

The Aliens Act of 1905 that followed marked a significant break in the liberal tradition with respect to the movement of people into Britain. The right of political asylum was preserved, but unrestricted entry was abrogated and some controls were introduced for the categories above. There was a marked decline in Eastern European immigrants in the years immediately after 1906, but after a low point in 1909, Jewish immigration increased again to reach 5,000 a year by 1914, which in fact had been the average between 1881 and 1905.

The Sydney Street Siege

In 1910, immigration was still a hotly debated political topic that from time to time became acrimonious. *The Times* alleged that the Houndsditch district 'harboured some of the worst alien anarchists and criminals who seek our too hospitable shore'. There undoubtedly existed among the immigrants those who covered a full spectrum of revolutionary aspiration, though they were very much a small minority who could be numbered only in the very low hundreds. (They are discussed in length in William Fishman's book, *Jewish Radicals*).

Pent-up emotions on the subject were released when on the evening of 16 December 1910 a suspicious neighbour heard what sounded like hammering noises from No.11 Exchange Buildings, Cutler Street, which adjoined a jewellery shop. He called the police, who were unarmed, and they were met by a hail of bullets as they entered the house. Three police officers were killed and two others seriously injured. The gang of four who were attempting to break through into the jeweller's shop from premises they had rented next door escaped, though their leader, George Gardstein, was mortally wounded and died shortly afterwards. Descriptions of the wanted men, with a reward of £500, were posted throughout the East End.

Sydney Street, Stepney.
Churchill attended the
scene of the seige wear-
ing a fur-collared coat
and a top hat.
(Courtesy Tower
Hamlets Local History
Library and Archives)

The press began an assault on anarchists and political refugees, lumping them together in an all-out anti-alien campaign. It was the biggest 'hue-and-cry' since the Ripper murders. Two weeks later, on 2 January, a Mrs Gershon living at No.100 Sydney Street in Stepney went to Arbour Square police station and reported that two men who had rented a room from her on the first floor answered to the description. She went back to the house and the men, sensing that they had been betrayed, deprived her of her skirt and boots on the assumption that no religious Jewess would attempt to escape in her underclothes. But Mrs Gershon was made of sterner stuff and went downstairs, where she was rescued by the police who had surrounded the house.

The police were armed with revolvers, shotguns and rifles but these proved completely inadequate for flushing out the gunmen, whose Mauser pistols, which they used freely, were capable of rapid and deadly fire.

Winston Churchill, the Home Secretary, was contacted, and permission was given to send for troops. Twenty-one volunteer marksmen of the Scots Guards arrived from the Tower of London. Three were placed on the top floor of a nearby building, from where they could fire accurately into the second storey and attic windows from which the gunmen had been shooting. The gunmen were driven down to the lower floors where they came under fire from more guardsmen positioned in houses across the street.

Against the advice of his officials Churchill, wearing a top hat and fur-collared coat, arrived on the scene before midday and took command. He decided that heavier artillery was needed, but before it could arrive smoke was seen rising from the building and one of the gunmen emerged from a window and then fell back suddenly. The building burst into flames, was soon gutted, and the roof caved in. Firemen were at work to prevent damage to other buildings when a wall collapsed, burying five people, one of whom died in hospital. Two bodies were discovered inside the house. It was, reported the police, a very rare case of a Home Secretary taking police operational decisions.

At 2.40pm, when it was evident that no one in the house had survived, Churchill drove off to a City restaurant for lunch. As he did so, a section of Royal Horse Artillery trotted up. This formidable reinforcement – two quick-firing 13-pounder guns with wagons and 20 rounds of shrapnel, came from the Battery's barracks in St John's Wood; the six-mile journey across London had been accomplished, it was said, in 40 minutes and without drawing rein.

The episode gave an opportunity to those who wanted stricter enforcement and extension of the Aliens Act to urge that further restrictions should be imposed, but in general all the political parties settled down to living with the Act. Churchill kept changes to a minimum and said he would resolutely refuse to withdraw the right of asylum, nor would he cause any unnecessary disturbance to the great bulk of the country's alien population, mainly Jews, which was in an overwhelming degree peaceful, hard-working and law-abiding.

After the start of World War One immigration stopped almost completely, though there was an influx of Jewish refugees from Belgium, many of them Polish by birth. There was no room at the Temporary Shelter that by now was in Mansell Street, and they were given the use of the former Westminster Union workhouse building in, appropriately enough, Poland Street in the West End. (They made a significant contribution to the orthodox community of Soho, and one of the children of this group of settlers, Rabbi Dr Isidore Epstein, was appointed principal of Jews' College in 1945).

Causes of conflict within the community

The mass immigration led to undoubted strains and friction within the community. Areas that caused serious tension and contention between the existing community and the newcomers were religious observance and the religious education of the young, the use of Yiddish, and the question of medical care.

Every Jew in the East End lived close to a synagogue. Over the course of the period 1880–1939 there were more than 120 in the area. Some streets had

*November 1889. A
typical scene in an
East End chevra.*

two, and they ranged from large synagogues such as the Great to tiny one-room affairs in a house. But they all had their officers, and the *shammas* (sexton) of the smallest synagogue was as proud of his position as the *shammas* of the greatest.

November 1889. A typical scene in an East End chevra.

Many newcomers considered the official religious organisations of Anglo-Jewry unsatisfactory both in their services and the religious instruction they gave to the children. They had weighed up the orthodoxy of the United Synagogue and found it wanting, and were prepared to openly repudiate it. The minority who were aware of the existence and beliefs of the Chief Rabbi had little regard for him and referred to him as the Chief Reformer. They came from self-governing communities, each with its own rabbi, and the Chief Rabbi's office was alien to their Eastern European experience. Many newcomers were reluctant to attach themselves to the existing synagogues.

They shunned the coldness of the lofty cathedral-like structures of the United Synagogue and the Reform Synagogue with their stained glass windows and massive pillars. In their eyes the English ministers were, in the main, men of little Jewish scholarship who were not sufficiently orthodox. The services did not have the warmth and fervour, the *heimische* (homely) atmosphere of a kind that they desired and to which they were accustomed. The ministers, in their long black gowns and white bands, had the appearance of non-Jewish clergy, particularly when they wore clerical collars. It was not surprising that the newcomers set up their own places of worship, in many cases improvised in a room or a house. These *chevrot* combined the function of a benefit club for death, sickness and the solemn rites of mourning, with that of public worship and the study of the Talmud. All were developed as a labour of love.

The *chevrot* were usually small, noisy, sometimes scruffy, and informal. They were frequently badly managed, fractious and chaotic; some slight difference of opinion between the members could lead to the formation of yet another *chevra* and then another. But they were open at all times of the day and, most importantly, the members felt comfortable and at ease in them. They came to these hotbeds of Judaism to pray, or study, or chat, or a combination of all three. They

Whitechapel and Mile End Station opposite the London Hospital. (Courtesy Tower Hamlets Local History Library and Archives)

came, wrote Israel Zangwill in *Children of the Ghetto,* 'two or often three times a day to batter the gates of heaven. They dropped in, mostly in their workaday garments and grime, and rumbled and roared and chorused prayers with a zeal that shook the window-panes. It supplied them not only with their religion, but their arts and letters, their politics and their public amusements. It was their home as well as the Almighty's'. It was, said Beatrice Potter, a touching sight to enter one of the poorer and more wretched *chevra* on a Sabbath morning. At the conclusion of the service:

> *... the women have left, the men are scattered over the benches (maybe there are several who are still muttering their prayers) or they are gathered together in knots, sharpening their intellects with the ingenious points and subtle logic of the Talmudic argument, refreshing their minds from the rich stores of Talmudic wit, or listening with ready helpfulness to the tale of distress of a newcomer from the foreign home.*

Many of these synagogues were named after the town or district in Russia or Poland from which the majority of its members had emigrated, such as the Sons of Lodz or Brethren of Konin and Kovna. The *Jewish Chronicle* stormed against them:

The minor places of worship ... originate partly in the aversion felt by our foreigners for the religious manners and customs of English Jews ... the sooner the immigrants to our shore learn to reconcile themselves to their new conditions of living the better for themselves. Whatever tends to perpetuate the isolation of this element of the community must be dangerous to its welfare ... they should hasten to assimilate themselves completely with the community amongst whom they dwell ... if they intend to remain in England, if they wish to become members of our community we have a right to demand that they show signs of an earnest wish for completely amalgamating with the aims and feelings of their hosts.

Polly Nathan's famous fried fish shop in Petticoat Lane. (Courtesy Tower Hamlets Local History Library and Archives)

One member of the Jewish elite who was particularly sympathetic to the problems of the newcomers was Sir Samuel Montagu (in 1911 he was elevated to the peerage as Lord Swaythling), the Liberal Member of Parliament for Whitechapel. A strong adherent to orthodox Judaism, he found much to admire in the *chevrot* and took steps to preserve them. His idea was to get rid of unsanitary places of worship and amalgamate the smallest into viable units in suitable buildings. In 1887 he merged 16 *chevrot* (including eight which were in existence before 1881) under the umbrella of a Federation of Minor Synagogues (the word 'minor' was soon dropped). Admission was refused to congregations of less than 50 members or to those which did not conform to the Federation's building requirements, until the defects were remedied.

One reason, but not the only reason, that Montagu established the Federation, was that he hoped that by strengthening the cause of religion among his religious immigrant constituents he would hold at bay the socialists whom he considered to be a growing danger. He also aimed to make the Federation an indirect method of integration, by appointing a minister, whose salary he met, and who would not only be a Yiddish-speaking Talmudic scholar but also one who could preach in English. 'We cater', said Montagu, 'for the working class amongst Jews'. When a testator left £4,000 to the 'London Synagogue for the Poor' both the United Synagogue and the Federation claimed the money. Unable to reach a settlement the dispute went to court and the Federation was adjudged to be the institution designated by the testator.

In 1894 the celebrated religious orator, Chaim Maccoby (1859–1916), known as the Maggid of Kaminetz, was appointed preacher to the Federation. His fiery emotive speeches calling for repentance, interspersed with stories, anecdotes and even jokes, drew large congregations. One who attended his sermons said that there was always a good attendance of women in the gallery. After some time one of them would start to sob at the sad tale he related, and this, like yawning, was infectious and soon had the rest of the gallery joining in. At this point the *shammas* would bang on the desk and call for silence. During an oration lasting an hour or two, or perhaps even longer, this would recur on several occasions. The greater the number of sobs, the more highly rated was the success of the sermon, as judged by both the congregation and the preacher.

The Federation became a distinct force in Anglo-Jewry, with a membership that rivaled in numbers that of the United Synagogue and, in its initial years, accepted the authority of the Chief Rabbi. When Montagu died in 1911 the Federation had 6,000 members in 51 constituent bodies.

Though immigrant parents were increasingly prepared to entrust the secular education of their children to the schools, many – perhaps a majority – were dissatisfied with the quantity and quality of the Hebrew and religious education they provided.

Instead, paying perhaps sixpence or one shilling a week, they sent their sons to the *chederim* (more often than not they consisted of just a room in the teacher's house), in which elementary Hebrew and religion were taught. They sprouted everywhere in the East End in, it was said, 'stables, garrets and every sort of unlikely place'. The 1898 *Jewish Year Book* noted six in Booth Street alone. They were frequently shabby, ill-lit and ill-ventilated. Nonetheless, many immigrant Jews sent their children to them and to the Talmud Torahs, institutions of more advanced learning, that were also proliferating in the East End. Despite allegations that *chederim* in the neighbourhood of Bell Lane, Wentworth Street, Fashion Street and Brick Lane were the cause of grave physical evils, and that their pupils were pallid, washed out, and robbed of their childhood because of the long hours spent in them, they remained popular with the immigrant parent. None of the efforts of the day schools and the classes of the JREB could entirely displace this preference, nor could the persuasion of Lord Rothschild, who wrote a circular letter, printed in English and Yiddish, to the parents of every child at the Jews' Free School:

*Whitechapel High
Street in 1914. Note
the carts carrying hay
bound for the Hay
Market. (Courtesy
Tower Hamlets Local
History Library and
Archives)*

Dear Friend,

*I know what love and devotion Jewish parents feel for their children
… but it has long seemed to me that you may be doing your children
harm by the over-zeal which prompts you to send them to the chederim for so many hours a day … many boys attend the chederim as early
as 7 o'clock in the morning and remain there till it is time to go to
school. Immediately school is over they return to the chederim and stay
there until 8 or 9 o'clock at night … I ask you, are you not expecting
too much of your children of tender age? Do not these long hours seriously injure their health … I earnestly beg of you, therefore, to take
my words to heart and withdraw your children from the chederim altogether, or at least reduce the hours which they attend. They will then
grow up healthy and strong, fitted in every way to pursue an
honourable career, and with a reasonable prospect of becoming good
and worthy English citizens.*

It was to no avail. The *chederim* and Talmud Torahs continued to exist until the dispersal of the East End Jewish community.

For most of the newcomers their first, and sometimes only, language was Yiddish, a remarkable composite tongue which in one place was a mixture of Polish and Hebrew, in another of German and Hebrew, in another of Latvian and Hebrew. The elite disliked Yiddish, a dislike stemming from the belief that its continued use could keep immigrants isolated from the English community. For Moses Angel it was 'an unintelligible language', redolent of all that he considered undesirable in foreign ways and habits. Weaning his pupils away from it as quickly as possible, and substituting well-spoken English, was seen as an essential first step. His successor, Louis Abrahams, continued Angel's campaign, and advised parents and pupils to discard Yiddish completely – 'that miserable

The Pavilion Theatre, Whitechapel – 'the Drury Lane of the East End' – was home to a thriving Yiddish theatre. (Courtesy Tower Hamlets Local History Library and Archives)

A production at the Grand Palais in 1944. (Courtesy Tower Hamlets Local History Library and Archives)

jargon which is not a language at all'. Samuel Montagu asked pupils to refuse to learn Yiddish from their parents; instead, they should teach their parents to speak English. Basil Henriques, the founder of the St George's Settlement, said he could not speak Yiddish and could not learn it, 'chiefly because I won't, for I consider it the duty of every resident alien to learn English'.

The efforts of the schools brought their reward. A reporter from the *Daily Graphic* who visited the Jews' Free School in 1895 wrote, 'When they leave, they all speak English with a regard for grammar and a purity of accent far above the average of the neighbourhood'.

Nevertheless, despite all attempts to discourage its use, shop signs, posters and advertisements were in Yiddish. It was used in shops, at work, at union meetings and among neighbours, friends and families.

The post-1880 immigrant wave reinvigorated Yiddish culture. There had been unsuccessful attempts in 1867 and 1878 to found a Yiddish newspaper; by 1910 there were six daily Yiddish papers in London. Few lasted long, although the *Zeit* survived until 1950.

There was a thriving Yiddish Theatre at the Pavilion at the corner of Vallance Road and Whitechapel Road, 'the Drury Lane of the East'. It opened in 1906 and was 'remarkable for the range of its repertoire, the versatility of its actors, and the enthusiasm of its audience'. Comedies and dramas, many based on the Jewish experience in the Pale, were performed; the productions also extended to opera by Verdi and plays by Shakespeare. It peaked in the 1920s but rapidly declined after the mid-1930s.

In 1912 Feinman's Yiddish People's Theatre, a large hall in Commercial Road, with accommodation for 1,500 people, opened. Capital for the venture had been raised by issuing 12,000 £1 shares in a company, most being taken up by the poor of the East End. It was intended to be a Jewish cultural centre for opera and drama. It started with a performance of *King Ahaz*, an opera by the Jewish composer Samuel Alman. A Yiddish version of *Rigoletto* followed. Unfortunately the cost of the lavish productions was not covered by ticket sales and the scheme soon foundered.

Regular Yiddish theatre continued at the Grand Palais in Commercial Road. It was given a temporary boost in 1944 with a production of an anti-Nazi play called *The King of Lampedusa*, by S.J. Harendorf, based on the true story of a Jewish RAF airman, Sgt Sydney Cohen, who single-handedly accepted the surrender of the Italian garrison on the Mediterranean island of Lampedusa, on which he had made a forced landing. The play broke all records for popularity and drew large non-Jewish audiences. The Grand Palais continued to

VAPOUR BATHS

Shevshick's Vapour Baths in Brick Lane. They guaranteed to cure lumbago, arthritis and most other known illnesses. (Courtesy Tower Hamlets Local History Library and Archives)

The sign above the entrance of the up-market Yiddish newspaper, The Jewish Post and Express, *which operated during the 1930s, its premises adjoining Bloom's restaurant in Whitechapel.*

operate until 1970 but on a limited basis, mainly for charities. Its brilliant but dwindling cast, led by Anna Tzelniker, then travelled and gave smaller-scale performances for Jewish audiences throughout the country.

A Yiddish theatre performance was more than a conventional drama – it was a celebration of a shared language, culture and identity. Attending such performances gave an added communal unity and cohesion to its immigrant audience who looked forward to the weekend performances 'as a pious man waits for the Sabbath'. But time was on the side of the opponents of Yiddish, who were to a great extent pushing against an open door. By the early years of the 20th century its use was in natural decline. Although some immigrants never learned English however long they lived here, those who could speak and understand only Yiddish represented a relatively small proportion of East End Jews.

The general hospitals, the medical missions and the London Jewish Hospital

In 1880 there was of course no National Health Service, but wide-ranging health services were available. London was generally better supplied with medical services than the rest of England, and the East End of London better supplied than the rest of London. If you had to be Jewish, poor, and ill, the East End was a good place to be.

In the midst of the Jewish East End stood the great London Hospital (now the Royal London), one of the foremost hospitals in the world. Instituted in 1741 it had from its earliest days provided for its Jewish patients to have kosher food; they were given an allowance of 2½d a day to purchase their own meat and broth. Over the next 200 years, and indeed until beyond the end of World War Two, the London Hospital met requests from the Jewish community for kosher food, Jewish wards, facilities for celebrating the Sabbath and Jewish festivals, special visiting hours, special arrangements for post-mortems, and even separate ice chambers for Jewish bodies. They engaged Jewish almoners, and on the death of a Jewish patient allowed *wachers* (supervisors of dead bodies until burial) into the wards. At any given time there were several Jews on its Board of Governors and House Committee, though there appears to have been a quota in operation; as one Jewish member died or retired he was replaced either the same year or the following year by another.

The Annie Zunz ward in the London Hospital, c.1914.

All these facilities involved the London in additional expense, so why was it so generous to its Jewish patients? The answer lies in the generosity of the Jewish establishment towards the hospital. The great voluntary hospitals, such as Guy's, Bart's, St Thomas' and the London, depended for their continued existence mainly on voluntary donations from the public, and these came principally from the rich. There were particularly strong ties between Nathaniel, the first Lord Rothschild, and Viscount Knutsford, the Chairman of the London from 1897–1931. Following the mass immigration of the 1880s Rothschild and Knutsford entered into an agreement – Knutsford said he would ensure that the London Hospital provided the poor Jews with every facility they could reasonably require, and Rothschild agreed to ensure that the wealthy Jews contributed handsomely to the hospital and covered the additional costs incurred. Both kept their word. The London provided the facilities just outlined, and wealthy Jews supported the London financially. Dr Eardley Holland, a consultant at the hospital, said in 1937 that he started his day at the hospital by lecturing to students in the Bearsted Clinical Theatre; proceeded to operate in a theatre provided by W.B. Levy; conducted pathological researches in the Bernhard Baron Institute; and attended patients in wards named after a Raphael, a Rothschild and a Stern. At the King Edward VII's Hospital Fund (now the King's Fund), of which he was a commissioner, the Samuel Lewis Bequest was one of the main sources of income. 'In proportion to their numbers', he said, 'Jewish people give far more to the hospitals in this country than do other people'. The agreement between Knutsford and Lord Rothschild served the London Hospital and its Jewish patients well. Similar unwritten arrangements were made by the Jewish establishment with other voluntary hospitals in London and elsewhere in the country, including the Brompton Hospital for Consumption and Diseases of the Chest, Charing Cross Hospital, the Metropolitan and the German Hospital.

LONDON HOSPITAL, E.

President:
H.R.H. THE DUKE OF CAMBRIDGE, K.G.

Treasurer:
JOHN HENRY BUXTON, ESQ.

An APPEAL for FUNDS is now made to carry on the work of this, the greatest Charity of the East End, in its present efficiency.

All who are willing to assist the Committee by Contributions are most cordially asked to promise to send a donation, or to become annual subscribers. Any subscription, however small, is most cordially appreciated.

£40,000 a Year is required from Voluntary Contributions.

THE LONDON HOSPITAL ASKS FOR HELP

BECAUSE—It is the Largest Voluntary Hospital—776 beds.

It treated 10,559 In-patients last year.
It treated 2,412 Children under 12 years of age last year.
It has special Wards for Jews—830 treated in 1895.
It is a Special Hospital for Women, Cancer, Stone, &c., &c.
Its assured Income is only £20,000 a year.
It relieved 154,617 Patients of the poorest class in 1895.
It is managed with the strictest economy.

All interested are cordially invited to visit the Hospital.

J. H. HALE, ESQ.   G. Q. ROBERTS, M.A.,
Chairman.   *House Governor and Secretary.*

Thus hospital services for poor Jews living in the East End were good for their time, but among the large body of Yiddish-speaking immigrant Jews were some who felt ill-at-ease in them. They believed that patients who felt comfortable in their surroundings were halfway to a cure, and that the only hospital in which they could feel like this would be one in which the doctors and nurses, the general staff and even the porters were Jewish; one in which Yiddish would be widely understood and spoken. The movement that led to the establishment of a Jewish hospital in the East End began in 1907. It became a rare example of wealthy Jews not only not helping to found such an institution, but actively working against it.

It was an unpropitious moment for the supporters of the scheme to start. As medicine, surgical techniques and equipment improved, so costs increased and patients' expectations rose. Voluntary hospitals were finding it increasingly difficult to cope with the demand for their services, and their financial state was parlous. Bed, ward and wing closures became commonplace in the first 30 years of the 20th century. At one stage the London Hospital could not pay its milk bills, and Knutsford threatened a complete closure of the hospital.

It was obvious at the beginning of the century that the great voluntary hospitals could not survive in their existing form without considerable municipal or state assistance, or even a state takeover. So when, in 1907, an East End barber called Isador Berliner and a few of his working-class friends met in a basement flat in Sydney Street and announced they were intending to raise sufficient money to build and maintain a voluntary hospital close to the London Hospital, it seemed a ludicrous undertaking, particularly as it soon became clear that Lord Rothschild opposed the scheme. He did so partly because of his agreement with Knutsford; partly from fear that Jewish contributions to the London and the other voluntary hospitals would decrease and that this would lead to a diminishing service to their Jewish patients; and partly because he thought it was an unnecessary and divisive move. He resolutely set his face against it, and influenced his wealthy friends to oppose the scheme too. Not a single wealthy member of the community came to the aid of these working men. The Jewish clergy were also against them, as, initially, was the *Jewish Chronicle*.

After a long and gruelling struggle, facing many setbacks, the barber and his friends succeeded against all the opposition, raising the necessary capital in donations from the East End poor. At their first meeting they collected the princely sum of 1s 6d, but they persevered. As L.J. Greenberg, the editor of the *Jewish Chronicle*, described it:

> *They had to work and labour and strive and contrive for pennies and halfpennies and farthings, to canvass from house to house, night after night, in storm, in rain, in tempest or when the atmosphere in the alleys and byways they visited was well-nigh asphyxiating.*

It was not until 1919 that they were able to open the out-patient department, and not until 1921 that the hospital was fully operational. Berliner was elected president, but its first chairman, appointed in 1919, was Nathaniel's son, the second Lord Rothschild. With him on board, the money flowed in. The hospital was taken over by the National Health Service in 1948 and eventually closed its doors in 1979.

The efforts of Christian organisations seeking to convert Jews by opening schools in the Jewish area has been referred to, but it was their medical missions that caused the greatest heartache for the Jewish community. They made no secret of their objective. Their journal, *The East End Mission*, said:

> *The sole aim of our medical work is to lead these people from Judaism to the light of the Gospel, and to heal the disease of the soul through curing the sickness of the body. Hundreds owe their conversion to the Providence which, working through their sickness, brought them to the Medical Mission.*

In 1891, the London Society for Promoting Christianity among the Jews acquired premises in Goulstone Street for what was described as 'aggressive evangelistic work'. In his history of the Society, Revd W.T. Gidney wrote:

> *With thousands of Jews on every hand, it was admirably suited for this purpose, being in the midst of the dense and poor Jewish population of the East End, chiefly hailing from Russia and speaking Yiddish. The combination of a medical missionary organisation, with efforts of a more direct spiritual character, had tended to make the work very effective and telling.*

At different times during the period 1880–1935, there were at least nine medical missions in the Jewish East End, including those in Fournier Street, Whitechapel Road, Cambridge Road, Commercial Road, Buxton Street and Philpott Street.

A correspondent of the *Jewish Chronicle* said those who attended 'had first to hear a lengthy sermon preached against our religion, which is held to ridicule, to which they listen in silence, afraid to say a word against the sermon for fear of not being able to see the doctor', and sometimes the doors were locked so that they could not escape it. According to a report in the *Jewish Chronicle* of 12 December 1913, every morning at about 8.30am, and every afternoon at about 1pm, there was a large crowd, 99 percent of whom were Jewish, outside the doors of the Philpott Street Mission. Its staff consisted of two full-time doctors, two part-time doctors, a dentist, a consulting dentist, three lady dispensers, and three assistants. A Yiddish-speaking nurse was always available. It was open every day of the week until 3pm and a number of patients were allowed to recuperate at the Mission's Convalescent Home at Brentwood in Essex.

The missions were undoubtedly popular. Many East End Jews could not afford the 'sixpenny doctors'; resented the long waiting time in the hospital out-patient departments; and were unhappy at the thought of undergoing a searching and sometimes unpleasant inquiry from a parochial Receiving Officer. Mission doctors won their faith, and enjoyed a reputation for skill. They did not hurry the patients, and allowed time for general conversation and sympathy. Importantly, they were an additional source of treatment. Many Jews, (and non-Jews), went from hospital out-patient department, to a free dispensary, and to a doctor, all for the same complaint, taking a bottle of medicine from each, imbibing a spoonful from one in the morning, from another in the afternoon, and from the third in the evening. One witness to a United Synagogue Inquiry in 1912 into the work of the missions, said that if a fresh batch of doctors came into the East End they would all find work, and none of the existing doctors would suffer. The Jews would consult both.

East End Jews appear to have had few qualms about availing themselves of the missionaries' medical care – they took the leaflets, listened to the prayers and sermons (although some women stuffed their ears with cotton wool so that they should not hear the name of Christ), and departed none the worse for wear. All the evidence indicates that there were very few true converts.

The Jewish East End

Despite its disadvantages – and they were many – the East End was well provided with the necessities of Jewish life and death; several scores of synagogues, Jewish schools, shopkeepers selling kosher food and four burial grounds within easy distance. In Petticoat Lane, Wentworth Street, and Brick Lane there was scarcely a shop or stall that was not Jewish-owned. Streets were thronged with Jewish shoppers, and contained everything for the Jews' daily needs, the small grocery shops reeking of pickled herring, garlic sausage and onion bread. It was also an area full of meeting places – Jewish clubs, societies, cafés and restaurants – a self-contained milieu that encompassed a whole range of social and cultural life in which people spoke of Warsaw, Kishinev, Kiev, Kharkov and Odessa as if they were neighbouring suburbs. 'I doubt' said one observer, 'if there is any place in the wide world that contains so much of intense human interest as exists in Whitechapel'.

Fine Georgian houses in New Street.

Russell and Lewis, in their 1900 book *The Jew in London*, noted that alongside the over-crowding, the most conspicuous features of this Jewish colony were sobriety and hard work:

Strange as it may seem, this great and largely squalid colony is a peaceful and law-abiding population. On the larger scale it may even be said to be a moral population ... Personal violence towards women is almost unknown. Licentiousness among women is equally rare. Family ties are sacred. Considering that Whitechapel is overwhelmingly a colony of aliens, the consequences, socially and politically, might have been serious, a disaffected people might have been a standing menace to London ... Happily, nothing, in fact, is more remarkable on Sunday than the orderliness of a great population of aliens in faith and speech ... who are, it must be said, less aggressive in the streets than many of their better circumstanced co-residents.

The streets of the East End provided a fascinating and exciting mixture. The broad promenade of Whitechapel Road, one of the widest in London, was the gathering ground, breathing space, market and discussion forum of the immigrant Jews – 'a great living picture gallery of the street scenery of our Eastern Babylon.' Off Whitechapel Road, at every quarter mile or so, was an unusual side street to catch the interest, such as Black Lion Yard, with so narrow an entrance that you would pass it 20 times and not know it was there. But enter it, and you would find that almost

The Cloth Market in Goulston Street, early 20th century. (Courtesy Tower Hamlets Local History Library and Archives)

every shop was a jewellery shop, the providers of engagement and wedding rings for the community. And in the middle of the jewellery shops a herd of cows – a kosher dairy farm.

The streets throbbed with life. 'Whitechapel on a fine Sunday evening is like Blackpool front in August. All the shops are open, and the restaurants busy. It is a fashion parade of youths and girls in smart clothes, and strolling elders not so smart'.

Jewish friendly societies

Friendly societies, which almost every family joined, gave help when it was most needed, in times of sickness, death or unemployment. Each society had its full quota of officials, with Presidents and Vice-Presidents, Secretaries and Finance Officers, committee members and collectors, and proper minutes kept and meetings meticulously recorded (sometimes). They gave many a position of responsibility and respect in the community, and a feeling of belonging. Some Jewish fathers made it a condition of giving their consent to the marriage of their daughters that prospective sons-in-law should join a friendly society.

By 1911 there were 25,000 individual members of Jewish friendly societies, contributing an average 2d per week for medical benefit. Most societies gave full sickness benefit of 15s per week for about 13 weeks, and half that for the next 13 weeks. Members had the services of a doctor, and many Jewish general practitioners in the East End derived their staple income from their contracts with friendly societies.

On average, Jewish friendly societies gave higher medical benefits than the non-Jewish societies. During the passage of the Insurance Bill through Parliament, the Federation of Jewish Friendly Societies secured changes to clauses that would have caused hardships for aliens who constituted a high proportion of their membership. They achieved this by convincing Lloyd George that overall Jewish societies paid out, per member, less in sickness benefit than the general societies. From this it was argued that Jews would be less of a burden on the National Insurance Scheme than the rest of the general public. How could Jewish societies pay higher benefits, and yet spend less per head? The answer was partly that there were fewer sickness claims by members of Jewish societies, but detailed examination revealed that much of the difference was accounted for by the duration of the claim for sickness benefit – Jews seemed to throw off sickness more quickly than non-Jews. It is of course possible that the figures reflected a different attitude to work, and the return to it after illness, rather than a quicker recovery time.

Because Jewish societies paid out less for sickness benefit, they achieved surpluses that were used to improve other benefits – such as disablement and maternity benefits, and payment for consultations with specialists. Some societies also paid for nursing, dental, and hospital treatment.

The clubs

In addition to the effects of the compulsory system of national education, there were other activities either directed principally towards integration or incidentally promoting it. The community encouraged the setting up of a network of clubs and societies catering for both adults and young people, all of which had the underlying aim of 'ironing out the ghetto bend'.

The Jewish Working Men's Club, founded in 1872, moved to a new building in Great Alie Street in 1883 and had facilities for 1,300 adult members and 300 youths. The West Central Jewish Boys' Club was founded in 1895, followed by the Brady Boys' Club in 1896. The latter's stated aim was 'to establish a social and recreational centre for working lads fresh from school, to improve their stunted physique, raise their general tone and bearing, inculcate into them habits of manliness, straight-forwardness and self-respect'. That was largely the aim of the other youth clubs in their early days. In 1903 three-quarters of the boys at Brady were children of foreign parents. Most were found apprenticeships through the Board of Guardians, which

Cutler Street, the scene of the attempted robbery that led to the Sydney Street Siege. It continued as a Sunday jewellery market until after World War Two.

advanced their apprenticeship premiums and allowed them to be paid back in easy instalments. Conversation at the club was in English and the games arranged, as at the other clubs, were the normal English sports – cricket, football, swimming. The Jewish Girls' Club was formed in 1886, the West Central Jewish Girls' Club in 1887, and the Stepney Jewish Lads' Club opened at the end of 1900.

The clubs played their part in the process of integration. Jewish youths, while rarely resorting to violence, were often self-assertive, noisy, obstreperous, slow to respond to discipline and obstinate. The Bishop of Stepney once felt moved to write to the Chief Rabbi about their behaviour, suggesting that something be done to keep them occupied in industrious pursuits 'for their edification, enlightenment and upbringing'.

Oxford and several public schools had by then established numerous settlements in the East End, and it occurred to the Chief Rabbi that Clifton College, Bristol, which had a Jewish house, might be persuaded to start a settlement for Jewish lads. He put the idea to Revd Pollack, the master of the Jewish house:

> It seems to me that if some magnanimous benefactor suitably motivated could be found to provide the wherewithal for this worthwhile and necessary venture that our boys and past scholars might be encouraged to do their social duty towards their less fortunate brethren in the East End.

The result was the Victoria Club, founded in 1901. It was run by unpaid managers, prosperous young men with earnest intentions from the older families, who kept a detailed progress report:

> With time one notices progress in other directions. The reading room is more used, but then an old Jewish complaint raises its ugly head. Two visitors, J. Finklestein and A. Cohen, introduced the noble game of toss ha'penny into the club. We lectured the gentlemen on the iniquities of gambling and thereupon they announced their intention of foreswearing the sport.
>
> Careful attention is paid to the effects of cricket and there at first the results were not entirely heartening. There is still too great a tendency to squabble and play selfishly, also a disinclination to recognise the captain's authority. The situation improves with time but not entirely so.
>
> Very successful day of cricket. The behaviour of the boys in the field was good, but there is still a tendency not to accept the umpire's decision as final.

The largest and most successful of the Jewish settlements, Oxford and St George's, was founded shortly before the outbreak of World War One by Sir Basil Henriques (the street in which the club stood was named after him). Henriques worked for a time in Toynbee Hall and saw for himself the effects which poverty and overcrowding were having on Jewish youngsters in the neighbourhood.

The boys idolised him. Fair haired and over six feet tall, he had a commanding presence and a commanding voice. He loved sportsmen and sportsmanship and doing his bit (and more than his bit) for others, and the boys followed his lead.

The Jewish Lads' Brigade (JLB) was formed in 1895 and held its first summer camp in 1896. Colonel A.E.W. Goldsmid, an ex-Indian army officer, who came from the same ruling Anglo-Jewish clan as Henriques, founded the JLB, a sort of pre-Baden Powell Scout group, in 1896. He said:

We should endeavour to instill in the rising generation all that is best in the English character, namely independence, honour, truth, cleanliness, and love of active health-giving pursuits.

There was an implication in his statement that the ghetto boy was devoid of such virtues, but also a belief that there was little wrong with him that the influence of Englishmen and England could not put right.

A non-Jewish headmaster described it as 'an admirable movement for developing the physique, for inculcating habits of obedience and self-restraint, and for fostering a spirit of true patriotism'.

The Association for Jewish Youth was formed in 1909, and in particular arranged sport on Sundays.

The Jewish Dispersion Committee

Because of concern that the concentration of Jews in such a small area would encourage anti-Semitism to flourish and provide anti-alienists with the ammunition they needed to stop the flow of immigration, the Cousinhood adopted a strategy that was an attempt to disperse the community more widely, to empty the 'ghetto'. Offices were established to assist immigrants to settle in other areas, and attempts were even made to colonise Jews on land near Colchester where they would raise cattle and sheep to provide meat for the kosher market. Under the patronage of Samuel Montagu, the Jewish Dispersion Committee was established in 1903 with the aim of transplanting some of the more anglicized immi-

Providence Place,
1905. An alley to the
south of Whitechapel.

grants to smaller cities, such as Reading, where Jewish communal facilities existed.

There was really little need for the Dispersion Committee, because the immigrant quarter carried within itself the seeds of its own dissolution. Its very disadvantages – overcrowding, lack of open space, noise and congestion of streets, impelled residents to move as soon as they could. Although initially most new immigrants naturally tended to settle where their co-religionists already were, that is in the East End, most of them determined to leave as soon as their circumstances permitted it and to move out to the more spacious and healthier suburbs. By 1914 the Jewish population of the East End had declined by 25,000, from 125,000 a decade earlier to 100,000, and that owed very little to the efforts of the Dispersion Committee.

When the immigrants did leave, they followed a limited number of routes – north to Dalston and Hackney and then into Islington, Canonbury and Highbury; north-west into Hampstead, St John's Wood, Cricklewood, Willesden and Golders Green. To the north-east they went to Leyton, Walthamstow, East Ham, Manor Park, Forest Gate and Ilford, and also westwards to Notting Hill Gate, Ealing and beyond. There were smaller numbers to be found south of the Thames in New Cross and Brixton.

By 1914, the effects of immigration, early marriage and higher than average birth rates had led to a five-fold increase in the Jewish population of Britain from 60,000 in 1880 to 300,000, approximately what it is today, 93 years later. Immigration was reduced to a trickle during World War One, and the movement out of the East End accelerated. Through acculturation and social mobility the immigrants were clearly taking their place alongside the established community and its leadership.

The working-class element was steadily improving its working and living conditions, and the number calling upon assistance from the Jewish Board of Guardians was beginning to reduce. The number of professionals – barristers, solicitors, physicians, architects, engineers and some civil servants – continued to increase. It was not unusual for sons, and occasionally daughters, of the anglicised upper middle class to go to university, but what was significant was how soon the children of the newer immigrants, some born abroad, joined in the process. An outstanding example was Selig Brodetsky, who started at JFS and became a community leader as well as a distinguished professor at Leeds University. These developments were symptomatic of the successful integration of the new immigrants into Anglo-Jewry and British society.

By 1914, the community had come full circle and regained its stability. Compared to the position in the immediate aftermath of the events of 1881, the future looked bright.

Chapter 7

1914–1945: The Two World Wars

World War One

WHEN BRITAIN went to war in 1914 Anglo-Jewry responded to the call to arms. The *Jewish Chronicle* displayed a banner outside its offices in Finsbury Square proclaiming 'England has been all she could be to the Jews. The Jews will be all they can be to England'.

The Jews' patriotism was genuine, unambiguous and deeply felt, and had been instilled into Jewish youth in the schools and the clubs. The war provided an opportunity to disprove the charges of disloyalty and cowardice made by anti-Semites. The extent of the Jews' Free School's efforts were reflected in former Jews' Free School pupils' involvement in the war. More than 1,200 enlisted and suffered their share of death and injury while on active service, including the headmaster's son. The youngest volunteer was Joseph Rosenbloom, who joined the London Welsh Regiment in September 1914 when he was 13 years and nine months old, by lying about his age. He was wounded in action in Turkey before being discharged when his father informed the Army authorities of his age. 'One point in his favour must be mentioned', recorded the school magazine, 'When the recruiting officer asked if he was married or single, he told the truth'.

The Royal Navy would not take the foreign-born or those whose parents were born abroad, and there were only 400 Jewish naval ratings. In all about 14 percent of the Jewish community served in the armed forces as compared to 11½ percent of the British population generally. This favourable figure might be partly explained by the Jewish community having a disproportionate number of younger men. Five Jews were awarded the Victoria Cross. Three

THE COLOURS OF
THE 38TH (JEWISH BATTALION)
THE ROYAL FUSILIERS
WHO FOUGHT UNDER
THE BRITISH FLAG FOR
THE REDEMPTION OF
THE HOLY LAND IN THE
GREAT WAR 5674-9 1914-8.

אחד מדגלי הגדודים העברים
אשר נלחמו בבא בריטניה
בעד שחרור ארץ־ישראל
במלחמה הגדולה
ח' ער' תרעם

A commemorative tablet attached to the colours of the 38th Jewish Battalion of the Royal Fusiliers that were displayed in the Great Synagogue.

thousand lost their lives and 7,000 were wounded.

In the years following 1918 the community changed from being predominantly European-born to being predominantly British-born, partly because there was little immigration during and after the war. It was not until the 1930s that there was any further appreciable inflow.

The process of upward social mobility among the children of the immigrants of the 1880s continued, in occupations, social class, areas of residence and education. By 1939 perhaps 50 percent of them were moving steadily towards the middle-class category. In contrast, members of the Cousinhood, who had provided the community's leaders, had been weakened by the scale of their human losses during the war and a comparative reduction in their wealth. They could not be quite so prominent in their charitable giving, whereas those who had built up fortunes in retailing and light industry could.

This led to a gradual change in the balance of power between the old and the new families, but in an evolutionary rather than a revolutionary way. The 1920s and 1930s marked the beginning of the transfer of communal authority from the old, anglicised Cousinhood to a newer group of middle-class first and second-generation immigrants. In communal affairs the Board of Deputies remained the main representative body, the United Synagogue the largest religious body, and the Board of Guardians the leading social welfare organisation. Even though a majority of their leaders still came from the families who had controlled them before 1880, at a slightly lower level the children of the immigrants were beginning to make their way. The election of the Ukrainian-born Professor Selig Brodetsky as President of the Board of Deputies in 1939 was a significant landmark in the changeover of control.

The Brady Girls' Club based in Hanbury Street in the 1930s. (Courtesy Tower Hamlets Local History Library and Archives)

Zionism

The first organisation established in England that could perhaps be called

Cheshire Street Baths. The public baths were a necessity in an area with few bathrooms in private houses.

Zionist was the *Hovevei Zion*, 'Lovers of Zion', a movement begun as a reaction to the May Laws of 1882 and the pogroms in Russia. Its aim was to encourage the colonisation of Palestine. There were branches ('tents') in the provinces, but the largest was in London, which in 1893 had over 1,500 members, mainly immigrants. Its headquarters were at the School House in

Leading members of the community introduced to Theodor Herzl on his visit to London in 1895: the Very Revd Hermann Adler; the Haham Dr Moses Gaster; Sir Samuel Montagu (later Lord Swaythling); Lord Rothschild; Baron de Hirsch; F.D. Mocatta; Baron H. de Worms (later Lord Pirbright); Sir Benjamin Cohen; Dr M. Friedlander; Professor D.W. Marks; Sir Julian Goldsmid and Sir A. Sassoon. (Courtesy the Jewish Historical Society of England)

An early Zionist meeting in 1904, at which the lecture was in Yiddish.

Theodor Herzl at a meeting with English Zionists in 1896. Israel Zangwill and L.J. Greenberg are on his right, his mother is on his left, and Col Goldsmid is in front of her. (Courtesy the Jewish Historical Society of England)

Bevis Marks. The organisation managed to assist a few struggling settlements in Palestine formed by idealists from Russia and Romania, but it foundered at the turn of the century. Most of its members joined the English Zionist Federation that had been founded in 1897 as a branch of the World Zionist Federation.

Theodor Herzl (1860–1904) visited London in November 1895 and July 1896 to gather support for his dream of the creation of a Jewish national home in Palestine. On his first visit, just six months before the publication of *The Jewish State,* in which he outlined his programme, he became acquainted with several of the leaders of the Jewish community. He addressed the recently formed Maccabeans, a prestigious dining club of professional men, with Israel Zangwill in the chair. Personable, handsome and dynamic, Herzl made useful contacts. On a second visit he spoke to a different audience, a mass meeting of mainly immigrants at the Jewish Working Men's Club in Great Alie Street, whose president was Sir Samuel Montagu. Herzl's description of it was 'Packed. Fearful heat. Great jubilation'.

The overall reaction to his ideas was mixed. He made no great strides with the recent immigrants who were too busy trying to survive economically to have time for politics, and who in any event had no influence in the govern-

Itchy Park, in the churchyard of Christ Church, Spitalfields, derived its name from the tramps who gathered there before and after World War Two.

ment quarters that mattered. Some of the community leaders were concerned that the stress on a separate national identity for Jews might arouse anti-Semitism. However, his early supporters included Leopold Greenberg. When he became editor of the *Jewish Chronicle* in 1907 he turned it into a propaganda vehicle for Zionism. Israel Zangwill split off to found the Jewish Territorial Organisation, which sought an immediate home for the victims of Russian persecution. Chaim Weizmann (1874–1952) the first president of Israel, came to England in 1906 and became the leading Zionist. He recruited a group of young intellectuals, including Israel Sieff and his brother-in-law Simon Marks (both associated with the rising firm of Marks & Spencer), and Leonard Stein a barrister, and moved his base from Manchester to London. All worked tirelessly to promote the cause. While doing so Weizmann lived at No.67 Addison Road in London W14.

What really changed the overall situation was that Turkey, then in control of Palestine, joined World War One against the Allies. When General Allenby's forces ended 400 years of Ottoman rule in Palestine in 1917 Britain took charge of the country and became the central arena of Zionist activity. By this time the second Lord Rothschild had been converted to Zionism, and in June 1917 he and Weizmann saw Arthur Balfour, the Foreign Secretary, and told him that the majority of English Jews were in favour of the establishment of a Jewish state in Palestine. Thus it was that the Balfour Declaration of 2 November 1917 was delivered to Lord Rothschild at his Piccadilly address in the form of a letter from Balfour to Rothschild.

The movement of Jews away from the East End to the suburbs was of course just part of a general trend in London away from the city centre. The Jews favoured certain areas more than others. Between the wars the two main lines of development were along the commuter main-line railway to the east, to West Ham, Leyton and Ilford, of largely working and middle-class families. The other axis, predominately middle-class, was to Golders Green (which the underground had reached in 1907), Edgware, Hendon and Finchley. The property columns of the *Jewish Chronicle* in 1932 advertised houses in Golders Green, Edgware, Hendon, Cricklewood, Willesden, Stamford Hill, Dollis Hill, Harrow, Wembley Park, Northwick Park and Stanmore.

By 1930 barely one-third of London Jews lived in the East End and their numbers were diminishing steadily. Seven of the 11 elementary schools in the Jewish streets were no longer in use as schools, and by 1939 the roll of the Jews' Free School had fallen from its peak of 4,250 in 1900 to just 1,000 in 1939.

The Jewish West End

By contrast, it was not until the late 1930s that the Jewish population of the West End – Bloomsbury, Covent Garden, Fitzrovia, Soho, Marylebone and Mayfair – began to decline from the peak of about 30,000 that it had reached in the mid-1920s.

The experience of the post-1880 immigrants who came to the West End was similar to that of those who went to the East End. It was a close community and small enough for everybody to know each other, though there was the divide of Oxford Street. Some who lived to the south of it did not mix greatly with those living north, and each referred to those living 'on the other side', claiming the superiority of the side on which they lived. There was an abundance of synagogues, large and small, Jewish schools and Board schools with a predominantly Jewish roll, and a plentiful supply of butchers and grocers selling kosher meat and favoured Jewish delicacies.

Tailoring was the largest single occupation, but the quality of work was mostly of a higher grade as it was the West End Jewish tailors, many working from home, that made the garments for Savile Row and the stores in Oxford Street and Regent Street, including Peter Robinson, Gieves and Burberry. After World War One the area around the Middlesex Hospital became the headquarters of the ladies' clothing industry and continued so after World War Two, several of the top dress manufacturers having their showrooms in Great Portland Street. Others were engaged in street trading, and a high percentage of the shops in streets such as Berwick Street were Jewish-owned. There were also a surprising number of Jewish publicans, some of whom supplied thirst-inducing herrings, anchovies and pickled cucumbers free of charge.

Though crowded, and without the modern facilities nowadays taken for granted, the overwhelming recollection of those who lived there between the

The Bernhard Baron Settlement housed the Oxford and St George's Club, one of many highly successful East End Jewish youth clubs, c.1936 (Courtesy Tower Hamlets Local History Library and Archives)

wars was of a very warm, friendly, hard-working community. A fuller description of Jewish life in the West End can be found in the author's book *Living Up West*. The following extracts from interviews with inter-war West Enders give a flavour of life there:

I was an only child, but I had like 3,000 brothers and sisters. And, of course, there was Regent's Park, that was like a back garden.

My part of Soho was a village comprising Broad Street, Dufours Place, Marshall Street, Ganton Street and West Street, bounded by Carnaby Street at one end, then a rather quiet backwater, and the bustling market of Berwick Street at the other. Almost all the residents and shopkeepers in these streets were Jewish, and one knew the name of every single family who lived in them. Everything was within walking distance, shops, schools, and synagogues. A short walk took one to Oxford Street, Regent Street with its elegant shops, Shaftesbury Avenue, and Theatreland, with Piccadilly Circus the focal point, the flower girls with their baskets of multi-coloured flowers sitting on the steps of Eros.

In the summer, my mum used to get a box from Berwick Street Market and sit outside in the hot evenings with the other women to compare and watch the passers by. There was a lot going on. Our next door neighbours were tailors, and they used to work all night long. People would come up and talk to them while they were working.

When we went to Hyde Park on Sunday morning, it was a fashion parade. You wore a hat, gloves, and a mink tie with a head that clipped on.

The West End had many advantages. It was the centre of entertainment, culture, parks, squares, institutional headquarters, shops and restaurants, and the local Jewish residents took full advantage of it:

Where we lived we could walk into culture. We had access to the finest theatres, the finest plays, the music halls, variety shows, and concert halls. We used to go to the Old Vic and sit up in the gods. On Monday nights a big crowd of us used to go to the Palladium, about 30 or 40 of us; some paid and some forgot to pay. We met many a star, like Gracie Fields, and they would talk to all of us locals. We helped to make stars of them.

For the Jewish population of London generally there was a change in the occupational pattern. Tailoring was still important, but declining. The workshop-based boot and shoe trade and the hat and cap making trades lost their battles with the factories and by 1930 had almost disappeared. Female teenage manual workers moved on from the workshop to take up positions as sales assistants and clerical workers, though millinery and dressmaking were still popular.

During the war some Jewish manufacturers obtained government contracts for uniforms and boots for the services and many small workshop owners were able to expand, and a few became wealthy. During the war, labour was scarce and wages high, which led to a reduction in the numbers seeking relief from the Jewish Board of Guardians.

Occupations that grew after the war were upholstery, taxi driving and hairdressing, which gave scope for self-employment. The post-World War Two success of hairdressers such as Vidal Sassoon was a follow-on from this.

Boxing once again came into the limelight. There was an upsurge of professional Jewish boxers who supplanted the Irish as the dominant group in the ring. The Premierland in Whitechapel was a breeding ground for newcomers. Ted 'Kid' Lewis (born Gershon Mendeloff, 'the Aldgate Sphinx') won the British featherweight title in 1913 and the world welterweight championship in 1915. He was the first boxer to use a protective mouthpiece, designed for him in 1913 by his dentist, Jack Marks, now of course standard equipment in the sport of boxing. Jack 'Kid' Berg, 'the Whitechapel Windmill', won the British lightweight championship in 1934, defeating Harry Mizler, another Jewish boxer. Both 'Kids' became heroes, mobbed when they paraded around the streets of the East End following their triumphs in the ring.

The service industries were expanding and young Jews found work in family shops, and some then branched out on their own. The dance band era provided employment for Jewish musicians and there were many popular dance band leaders that older readers will remember, including Joe Loss, Geraldo, Harry Fox, Harry Roy, Maurice Winnick, Oscar Rabin, Ambrose, Sidney Lipton, Lou Praeger and Lew Stone. Also in the 1930s accountancy and estate agency steadily attracted Jewish entrants as a halfway house to the professions of medicine and the law.

Hitler and the English Blackshirts

In the 1930s, following Hitler's rise in Germany, there was a resurgence of anti-Semitism in Britain. The most active organisation was the British Union of Fascists, founded by Oswald Mosley in October 1932. Open allegations against Jews appeared in the party paper, the *Blackshirt,* and it concentrated its agitation in the East End of London. There were sporadic incidents of physical violence, particularly against the elderly, vandalism of synagogues and bricks through Jewish windows, stirred and agitated by speakers at street corner meetings in working-class areas.

At a Mosley rally, 12,000 strong, at Olympia on 7 June 1934, at which he

The crowds that gathered to stop Oswald Mosley's march through the East End on 4 October 1936. (Courtesy Tower Hamlets Local History Library and Archives)

launched a full-scale attack on the Jews, there were uniformed columns, Nazi salutes, and bands and flags copied from Nazi storm-troopers and Italian fascists. Hecklers were violently ejected.

As always when faced by such activity Jewish opinion was divided between those who advocated direct confrontation, meeting force with force, and those, such as the Board of Deputies, who believed such action inflamed the situation and made it worse. The Board preferred a political approach, co-operating with the Home Office and the Metropolitan Police Commissioner and relying on them to control it.

Mosley announced that in a show of strength he and his supporters would march through the East End on 4 October 1936. (A petition presented to the Government to ban the march was rejected as undemocratic). His uniformed supporters gathered at Tower Hill. When Mosley arrived wearing a black military-cut jacket, grey riding breeches and jack boots, and a black peaked military cap, his bodyguard alongside him in a van with barred windows, he was greeted with Fascist salutes. Escorted by motorcycle outriders he inspected his ranks, estimated at between 3,000 and 5,000.

Meanwhile, a large proportion of London's working class, men and women, Jews and Gentiles, dockers and garment workers, railwaymen and cabinet-makers, turned out in their thousands to thwart them. For hours every street between the Mint and Aldgate was thronged with people. Their slogan was 'They shall not pass'.

At the end of Cable Street, through which Mosley was due to march, barriers were erected of packing cases, an overturned lorry, a couple of carts, the contents of a builder's yard and anything else the crowd could lay their hands on. When the 5,000 police on duty tried to clear the barriers erected by the protestors they came into violent confrontation with the crowd in what came to be called the Battle of Cable Street. There were 87 arrests. The march was halted and the blackshirts had to alter their route. They went through the deserted streets of the City where they disbanded. On this occasion they were defeated and there was dancing in the East End streets that evening. A week later, a gang of 150 young Mosleyites smashed the windows of and looted 29 Jewish shops in the Mile End Road.

A ban on uniformed marches followed the events at Cable Street, and the Police Commissioner was given enhanced powers to control them.

Refugees from Nazi Europe

Events in Germany inevitably affected the situation elsewhere, and British Jewry was quick to recognise the implications of what was happening. The Board of Deputies set up a comprehensive committee structure to respond to various aspects of the challenge, and from the very beginning on behalf of Anglo-Jewry gave the Government a firm undertaking that no refugee Jew allowed into the country would become a charge on public expenditure, and that all expenses of their settlement would be borne by the Jewish community.

The Central British Fund for German Jewry was founded in 1933 and based at Woburn House in Russell Square. It was the financial instrument used to provide relief for victims of Nazism; the Jews' Temporary Shelter at No.63 Mansell Street and the Jewish Refugees' Committee at Bloomsbury House in Bloomsbury Street looked after their immediate needs.

A. Cohen, barber, of 71 Ellen Street, c.1930 (Courtesy Tower Hamlets Local History Library and Archives)

Fruit seller at 50 Old Montague Street 1935 (Courtesy Tower Hamlet Local History Library)

It was originally believed that no more than 3–4,000 German Jews would come, and initially the number was low. It was after Germany had occupied Austria in March 1938, and the dreadful events of Kristallnacht on 9 November 1938, when 269 synagogues, 1,000 Jewish shops and dwellings were burned and 30,000 arrests made, that emigration escalated. Thousands of Jews were thrown into concentration camps, and there were desperate attempts to flee. By the end of 1938 there were 38,000 German and Austrian Jewish refugees in Britain, and by 1940 about 73,000 had been admitted. Some later moved on, principally to the United States; it is

The public baths in Mile End.

Tombstone at Edmonton Cemetery of Dr Moritz Crunwald, former Chief Rabbi of Bulgaria, one of the many Eastern European rabbis who came as visiting rabbis to the East London Synagogues. (Courtesy David Jacobs)

Commercial Street in the 1980s.

estimated that 55,000 made Britain, and largely London, their permanent home.

They were in the main middle-class, urban, liberal and well-educated. They obviously did not need to adjust to western life, but had to make considerable adjustment to English life. Some who were used to a comfortable middle-class existence found themselves doing domestic work or sweeping factory floors. There was also a high proportion of children sent on their own. But as will be seen, the contribution that these refugees from Hitler, their children and grandchildren have made to British life has been exceptional.

There has been considerable discussion since the war and particularly in the past few years as to whether before and during the war Britain should have admitted more refugees and whether the Board of Deputies could have done more to persuade them to do so. What is beyond argument is that Britain accepted more refugees relative to the size of its population than other countries, including the United States, which had a far greater absorptive capacity.

World War Two

Virtually all Jews living in Britain in 1939 had been born in Britain (apart from the recent refugees) and were citizens and eligible for conscription. In all 60,000 served in the forces, including 10,000 in the Air Force and 1,500 in the Royal

Navy. 2,500 lost their lives. T.W. Gould was awarded the Victoria Cross.

In 1940 the Blitz heralded the physical end of much of the East End. Many communal buildings were destroyed by bombing, including the Great Synagogue in Duke's

A Stepney Green Queen Anne house in 1985. One of the East End homes at the upper end of the market.

Artillery Passage. A typical narrow alley-way once in Jewish but now in Asian occupancy.

The Grand Palais in Commercial Road kept the Yiddish theatre alive until the 1970s. (Courtesy Paul Raviv)

The Jewish Chronicle *centenary edition of 14 November 1941, with messages from the Prime Minister, the Chief Rabbi and the Archbishop of Canterbury.*

Place, and in the West End the Central Synagogue, the Western Synagogue and the adjoining Girls' Club, in which 16 club members died, were bombed. The last German rocket to hit London, in March 1945, fell on a residential block in Vallance Road and killed 130 victims, almost all Jewish.

In 1939, the East End still had the largest concentration of Jews in London, some 60,000. However, many evacuees and servicemen did not return to their homes, and by the end of the war the local community was reduced to 30,000. The decline was irreversible and continued at a rapid rate. By the 1990s there were no more than 7,500 Jews living in Whitechapel, Bethnal Green and Stepney. Today the figure is probably 3,000 or less. Some pockets of poverty remained; in the 1950s, the Soup Kitchen in Brune Street was still supporting 1,200 families, but it finally closed in 1992. When Bloom's, the well-known kosher restaurant in Whitechapel, closed its doors in 1996 it seemed as though the history of the Jewish East End had come to a symbolic end.

There has in recent years been considerable regeneration of the whole area, taking the best advantage of its proximity to the City and its banks and finance houses. Streets that the post–1880 immigrants sought to leave as soon as they could now have flats and houses in the £250,000 to £500,000 range and beyond. Many of their children, grandchildren and great-grandchildren could not afford to live there today.

Fashion Street. Note the solidly built houses with high-ceilinged rooms.

Chapter 8

1945–2007:
Anglo-Jewry Today

Education

In 1939, as war approached, Jewish education in London was in a sorry state, serious enough to be considered a danger to the communal future. Only half of school age children in greater London were receiving Jewish religious instruction, and the majority of them did so only after school hours.

Of the voluntary schools, the Jews' Free School had less than 1,000 pupils, and the Stepney schools were underpopulated. It seemed likely, because of the shifting pattern of London Jewish migration, that the Jews' Infants Schools, the Borough School in South London and the Westminster Jews' Free School

Bethnal Green Road with St Paul's Cathedral clearly visible, illustrating the close proximity of the East End to the City.

were coming to the end of their natural lives. The Solomon Wolfson School in Bayswater had accommodation for up to 500, but the attendance was only 200, of whom 10 percent were non-Jewish. There was an independent day school, the Jewish Secondary School, founded in 1929 by Rabbi Dr Victor Schonfeld in Finsbury Park and run after his death by his son, Solomon Schonfeld. In 1939 it had a boys'

school in Amhurst Park and a girls' and a primary school in Stamford Hill, collectively known as the Jewish Secondary School Movement (JSSM).

The JSSM placed special stress on Jewish studies in the orthodox tradition and most of its pupils were refugees from Nazi-occupied countries.

Wartime evacuation plunged many Jewish children into a non-Jewish home life, and the Jewish education of children during the war was reduced to a minimum despite the best efforts of communal organisations.

At the war's end all the day schools, apart from Stepney Jewish, Solomon Wolfson, the JSSM schools, and the Yesodeh Hatorah, orthodox schools founded in Stamford Hill in 1943, had been destroyed, damaged or closed down. It became clear that because of bomb damage and the moving away of most of their pupils, the Borough School and Westminster JFS would not reopen. It seemed highly doubtful, and subsequently became certain, that the Jews' Free School would not reopen at Bell Lane. It was against this general background that the gigantic task of the reconstruction of Anglo-Jewry's educational system began.

It was decided that the JFS, the Westminster JFS, the Jews' Infant Schools and the Borough Schools would realise and then combine

Prescott Street. There were many fine houses in the East End amid the overcrowded dwellings.

Hessel Street. After World War Two the Jewish shopkeepers left to be replaced mainly by Asians.

Whitechapel High Street in 1985. (Courtesy Tower Hamlets Local History Library and Archives)

The Hebrew Christian Testimony to Israel in Whitechapel, one of the many conversionist institutions in the East End. (Courtesy David Jacobs)

their assets, and use them to help establish new schools. The assets of the JFS, which included its freehold site and war damage claim, were far greater than those of all the other schools combined. Nonetheless, its governors generously agreed to put its assets into the pool for the general good, provided that sufficient funds were made available for them to replace Bell Lane. The surplus after that was reserved for fresh developments.

There was a considerable delay in implementing the plan because Dr Schonfeld of JSSM considered he should be put in charge of the fund. Eventually a compromise was reached; the JSSM received a sum of money from the fund. The Jews' Free School reopened its doors on a new site in Camden Town in 1958. It was an immediate success, has ever since been oversubscribed, has always achieved excellent academic results, and received many accolades. In 2002 it moved into a magnificent new building in Kenton that can cater for 2,000 pupils. Its headteacher, Ruth Robins, was made a Dame in the 2003 Honours List.

The JSSM schools, now known as the Hasmonean, are in Hendon and have facilities to educate children from the ages of 2–18. In the 2003 'A' Level exams it was the highest placed comprehensive school in the country. The community has four further secondary schools, in Redbridge the King Solomon School, in Finchley Pardes House Grammar School, in Stamford Hill the Yesodeh Hatorah has a secondary school to complement its primary schools, and in

Fieldgate Mansions. A typical East End housing block, 1990. (Courtesy David Jacobs)

The offices of the Federation of Synagogues in Leman Street, 1972. (Courtesy Paul Raviv)

The Davenant Foundation School, Whitechapel. One of the East End grammar schools that Jewish pupils first began to attend from early in the 20th century. (Courtesy David Jacobs)

Bushey Immanuel College is an independent mixed selective school.

It is at the primary level that there has been particularly strong growth with several new schools opening in many parts of the capital. Stepney Jewish

Schools moved to Ilford, and there are now more than 20 kindergarten and primary schools, liberal, reform and orthodox, spread through the areas of Jewish residence. Though the community as a whole is declining in numbers, a very high percentage of children of school age receive some form of Jewish religious education.

Welfare

Continuing in the age-old tradition Anglo-Jewry today has an enormous infrastructure of welfare bodies.

Jewish Care, effectively the successor to the 1859 Jewish Board of Guardians, is the largest provider of health and social care services for the Jewish community. It functions as an umbrella organisation catering for the elderly, the mentally ill, the physically disabled, the bereaved and the unemployed, as well as Holocaust survivors. Its resources include residential/nursing homes, day care centres, special day care centres, a youth and community centre, hostels, sheltered accommodation, social work teams and home care services.

Some of the excellent housing that was to be found in the Mile End Road. (Courtesy Tower Hamlets Local History Library and Archives)

The Jewish population is ageing faster than the general population so a higher proportion of communal expenditure has to be used to care for the aged. Jewish Care employs 1,500 staff and works in partnership with more than 2,500 volunteers. It strives tirelessly to streamline its own operations

and to encourage other Jewish welfare charities to do likewise and, where beneficial, to amalgamate and modernise and avoid overlapping.

The Jewish charities, like all other charities, have to deal with the growing gap between the money received from government and local authority sources and the actual cost of providing their services. They have to rely heavily on the generous support of the community at large to meet their annual obligations. Recent research revealed that 85 percent of London Jews had contributed to a Jewish charity in the previous year and 87 percent to a general charity. 68 percent had given more than £100, 11 percent more than £2,000 and two per cent over £10,000. With their help the Jewish charities manage to maintain their standards, but it is a constant struggle.

Immigration after World War Two

Since the end of the war the London community has been augmented by fresh arrivals from Hungary, India, Iraq, Egypt, Aden, South Africa and Israel. They probably did not exceed more than five or six thousand, but their

The entrance to what had been Chevrah Shass Synagogue. (Courtesy Paul Raviv)

South West London Synagogue in 1999. It had closed in 1997. (Courtesy David Jacobs)

Mile End and Bow District Synagogue, now a Hindu temple, 1997. (Courtesy David Jacobs)

South-East London Synagogue, now a Kingdom Hall of Jehova's Witnesses, 1990. (Courtesy David Jacobs)

impact on and contribution to London Jewish life has exceeded their numbers.

The 1956 Hungarian uprising brought several hundred additional members for the orthodox Adath movement in Stamford Hill. The two to three thousand

The synagogue at Shackwell Lane, Dalston, 1985. (Courtesy David Jacobs)

arrivals from India, Iraq and Egypt and the small group of Adeni Jews who came following Yemen's declaration of independence increased the membership of the comparatively small Sephardi community by 75 percent. There is a Persian and an Adeni synagogue in Stamford Hill. There has also been a fairly considerable inflow of Israelis since the 1970s, and many have opened Israeli-style restaurants and bakeries, particularly in the Golders Green and Temple Fortune areas.

Spitalfields Great Synagogue in 1968. (Courtesy Tower Hamlets Local History Library and Archives)

The Jewish population of London in 2007

The Jewish population of Britain peaked at about 425,000 in the early 1950s. Today, based on the figures disclosed by the 2001 census, the best estimate is that it now numbers about 300,000, of whom about 200,000 live in the extended London area. The fall is of course worrying for the community, and is reflected in the title of the Chief Rabbi's 1994 book, *Will we have Jewish grandchildren?*

The largest concentrations are to be

The Great Synagogue in 1972. The simple synagogue was erected to replace the original destroyed in World War Two. It closed in October 1958 because of declining membership. (Courtesy David Jacobs)

Interior of the New Road Synagogue in 1972 after being bought by a dress manufacturer. (Courtesy David Jacobs)

The young street trader, commonplace between 1850 and 1920, could still be seen post-1945 in the East End markets.

found in north-west and north-east London. They have spread beyond the pre-1939 boundaries, and gone deeper into Essex and Hertfordshire, with growing communities in such as Radlett, Bushey, Elstree, Borehamwood, Shenley, Chigwell, Cockfosters, Mill Hill, Pinner, Watford, Woodside Park, Potters Bar, Ruislip, Hatch End, Harrow, Wimbledon and Northwood.

The National Front has re-emerged, but much of its action is directed against coloured immigrants. Before the arrival of large numbers of immigrants from Africa, Asia, the Caribbean and Middle East, the post-World War Two make up of Britain's population was remarkably homogenous, and far more emigrated than entered the country. The Jews then stood out more. The new immigrants of the 1960s put Jewish identity in a new perspective. Britain is very much more a multi-cultural society. Jews constitute a far smaller minority than several of the succeeding immigrant ethnic communities, and it is noteworthy than a series of bomb attacks committed by one person in the 1990s was directed at the Asian, Gay and Black communities.

The latest research on the London Jewish community reveals that today it is comparatively affluent and middle-class. They have a higher than average involvement in medicine, accountancy, university teaching, law, dentistry, phar-

Far left: Poultry sellers.

Left: Wickhams department store, situated in the Mile End Road by Stepney Green, 'the Harrods of the East End'.

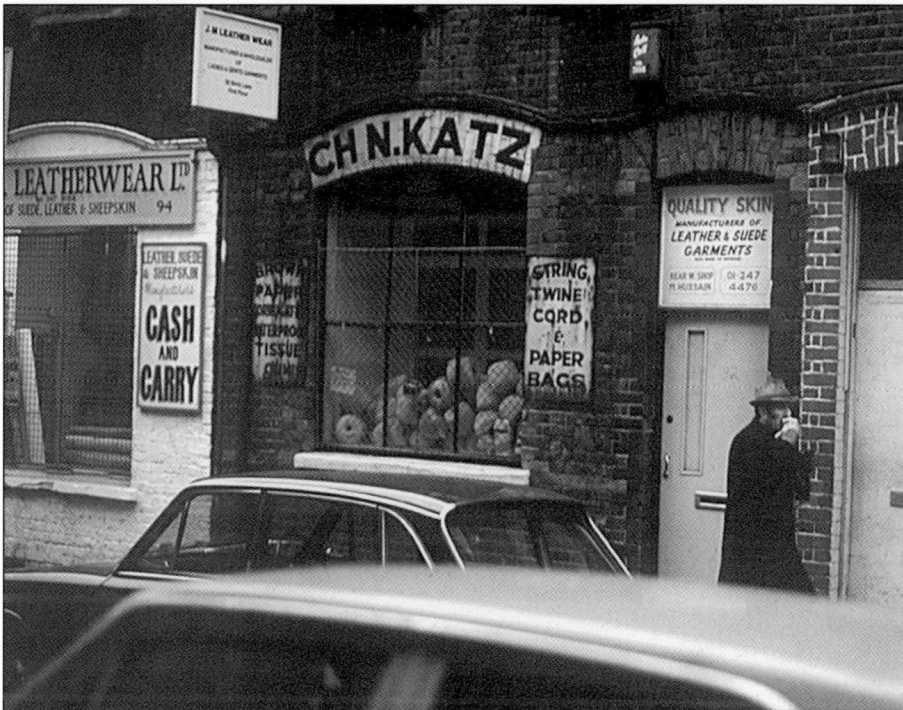

One of the dwindling number of Jewish shops still to be found in Brick Lane in the 1970s.

macy, estate agency and property. There has been a decline in shopkeeping, the Asians having taken their place in small family shops which, as happened with the Jews, sometimes blossom into chains. Generally speaking there are no occupations without a Jewish presence.

More of London's Jews describe themselves as secular than describe themselves as religious, but even among the secular there is a strong attachment to Jewish organisations. Rather than being a religious group they are an ethnic group within British society, with shared historical memories, common ancestry and an overall sense of solidarity.

They still like to be near the essentials of Jewish life, the synagogue, Jewish schools, kosher butchers and delicatessen shops that cater to their tastes. They prefer to live near other Jews. More than 80 percent in north-east London and

*An all-night beigal
shop on the corner of
Vallance Road and
Selby Street.*

*Tubby Isaacs. Jellied
eels are not kosher, but
Tubby's business
prospered nonetheless.*

90 percent in north-west London know of other Jewish residents in the same street, and more than half in those areas have a Jewish next-door neighbour. The more scattered nature of south London Jewry is illustrated by the fact that only 22 percent know of another Jewish resident in the street. Only three percent have a Jewish next-door neighbour.

There were still furniture makers in Bethnal Green after World War Two, though many had moved out to the Lea Valley.

Premises of Madame Yanovsky, the famous East End corsetière, in 1972. She later moved to Edgware Road. (Courtesy David Jacobs)

J. Samuel & Son, stone-masons who particularly catered for the Jewish trade.

A poultry dealer in Hessel Street in 1972, long after it had ceased to be a predominately Jewish market. (Courtesy David Jacobs)

Whether religious or not, more than 90 percent think it important for their children to meet in Jewish social groups. Of those surveyed 88 percent read the *Jewish Chronicle* either regularly or sometimes. More than half are involved in some type of voluntary work.

Whether the decline in numbers can be halted cannot be stated with certainty, but having enjoyed an unbroken presence in London for the past 351 years there is no reason to believe that the Jewish community cannot continue, and be successful, for the foreseeable future.

Appendix

In the year 2006, the Jewish community celebrated 350 years of Jewish life since the Resettlement with nationwide and local events. The Queen honoured the community with a reception at St James's Palace for 500 people chosen from all walks of life. She said the contribution of Jewish individuals and organisations to the national life over the centuries had been remarkable, and she appreciated their warm expressions of loyalty extended to her.

At the Mansion House, the City of London hosted a banquet at which Prince Philip was a guest of honour, the only person present who fifty years earlier had been at the 300th anniversary party. In his speech, Lord Levine, the former Lord Mayor, said that 'we are all hugely proud to be British Jews. I hope and pray that in 150 years' time in this amazing city there will be another great celebration like this'.

The Banquet at Mansion House.

© *Ian Lillicrapp*

In June, national and civic leaders of all parties and denominations attended Bevis Marks Synagogue for a service of thanksgiving. The Prime Minister said the Jewish community had been sustained, and its contribution underpinned, by the values for which it so strongly stands – the family, help for the needy, care for the sick, hard work and inventiveness, compassion and inspiration in equal measure – values which are also the best of what the United Kingdom stands for.

Henry Grunwald QC, President of the Board of Deputies, said the Jewish community had integrated fully with British society without losing its distinctive identity and 'there has been no area of British life to which the Jews have not contributed: arts and science, business and finance, industry and technology, medicine and law, academia and the media, politics and public services, including the armed forces, and importantly charitable giving'. To name individuals from the thousands deserving of mention risks omitting individuals who should be included, and would be an invidiuous task. A booklet, *Living and Giving The Jewish Contribution to Life in the United Kingdom*, sponsored by the Board of Deputies, has details of many of the deserving, and can be seen on-line at **www.britishjews350.org.uk.**

The Chief Rabbi Jonathan Sacks has written that immigration and acceptance take time, and that the best advice ever given to religious minorities was that of the prophet Jeremiah twenty-six centuries ago, when he told the Jews who had been exiled to Babylon: "Seek the welfare of the city to which you have been carried, and pray to God on its behalf, for if it prospers, you too will prosper".

Further reading

Bermant, Chaim, *The Cousinhood*, New York, 1971.

Black, Gerry, *Living Up West: Jewish Life in London's West End,* London, 1994.

—— *JFS, The history of the Jews' Free School, London since 1732*, London, 1998.

—— *Lord Rothschild and the Barber: The struggle to establish the London Jewish Hospital*, London, 2000.

Feldman, David, *Englishmen and Jews. Social Relations and Political Culture 1814–1914*, London, 1994.

Gartner, Lloyd, *The Jewish Immigrant in England 1870-1940*, 3rd edition, London, 2000.

Endelman, Todd M., *The Jews of Georgian England 1714-1830*, Michigan, 1999.

Lipman, V.D., *A history of the Jews in Britain since 1858*, London, 1900.

—— *The Jewish Board of Guardians: A Century of Social Service, 1859–1959*, London, 1959.

Mazower, David, *Yiddish Theatre in London*, 1987.

Pollins, Harold, *Economic History of the Jews in England*, London, 1982.

Renton, Peter, *The Lost Synagogues of London*, London, 2000.

Roth, Cecil, *A History of the Jews in England*, 3rd edition, London, 1964.

Rubinstein, W.D. *A history of the Jews in the English-Speaking World: Great Britain*, London, 1996.

White, Gerry, *Rothschild Buildings*, 1980.

Index